CAREY SCOTT

Clothe Your Heart in Love

ENCOURAGING DEVOTIONS
FOR A WOMAN OF GOD

BARBOUR
PUBLISHING

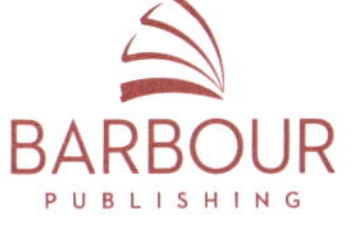

ISBN 979-8-89151-232-0

Cover Design: Greg Jackson, Thinkpen Design

Published by Barbour Publishing, Inc., 1810 Barbour Drive, Uhrichsville, Ohio 44683, www.barbourbooks.com

Our mission is to inspire the world with the life-changing message of the Bible.

Printed in China.

Introduction

God's greatest commands are to love Him and to love others. They are also the hardest! But as we grow in our faith and deepen our relationship with the Father, our desire and ability to love will flow from it.

Let this book help you understand what genuine and godly love looks like and how to walk it out in your life daily. Discover ways to express love powerfully, even when it feels difficult. Learn about God's love for you and how to accept it. Find meaningful ways to convey your love to the Lord.

As you turn each page, you'll be encouraged to embrace compassion in new and fresh ways. You will be challenged to think and act differently. If you allow it, clothing your heart in love will change your life.

When you ask,
God will mature your
ability to love patiently,
kindly, and humbly.

A Work in Progress

Love is patient; love is kind. Love isn't envious, doesn't boast, brag, or strut about. There's no arrogance in love.

1 CORINTHIANS 13:4 VOICE

The truth is that loving others is hard. No matter how we slice it, being caring and compassionate doesn't always come easily. But the Bible is very clear about how we are to treat others, whether easy or difficult.

Ask God to grow love within you so you're able to obey His command. Rather than feel like a failure when you mess up and aren't as patient and kind as you'd like to be, remember you are a work in progress. Choose to celebrate the accomplishments of those around you so jealousy can't tangle your heart and mind with unhealthy feelings and thoughts. Always be humble, never thinking you are better than others.

When you ask, God will mature your ability to love patiently, kindly, and humbly.

DEAR LORD, HELP ME GROW TO LOVE OTHERS IN THE RIGHT WAYS SO THEY ARE BLESSED AND YOU ARE GLORIFIED. IN JESUS' NAME, AMEN.

With Excellence, Not Perfection

Never haughty or selfish or rude. Love does not demand its own way. It is not irritable or touchy. It does not hold grudges and will hardly even notice when others do it wrong.

1 CORINTHIANS 13:5 TLB

How can you express genuine love to others when your words are rude and your demands are selfish? How can family and friends feel warm fuzzies from you when you're grouchy and moody? When you refuse to forgive and instead keep a scorecard of grievances, how are they to experience your kindness?

Be the kind of woman who loves others with excellence. . . not perfection. There will be times you get it very wrong—be it by accident or on purpose. You'll lose your cool, use hurtful words, entertain vengeful thoughts, and act in damaging ways. Your best efforts will fall flat. But in those moments, God will be there to convict and restore so you can apologize and rebuild.

DEAR LORD, HELP ME SHOW LOVE WITH EXCELLENCE, NOT PERFECTION. IN JESUS' NAME, AMEN.

Love for the Suffering

It isn't happy when injustice is done,
but it is happy with the truth.
1 CORINTHIANS 13:6 GW

When we love someone, it means we don't celebrate evil winning in their circumstances. When they lose or fail, or experience rejection or betrayal, we are burdened for them. We feel what they're feeling. Our heart breaks for what breaks theirs, and we stand with them as they navigate the fallout, seeking truth and healing from God.

Some people may secretly snicker, thinking they got what they had coming. They may feel superior because it didn't happen to them. But as believers, we should be flooded with compassion. We should be quick to come alongside those who are suffering. We should reach out to see how we can best support the hurting. Look for immediate and meaningful ways to express love.

DEAR LORD, OPEN MY EYES TO SEE WHEN OTHERS ARE SUFFERING, AND EMPOWER ME TO FIND WAYS TO SUPPORT THEM SO THEY FEEL LOVED. IN JESUS' NAME, AMEN.

Dependable Love

If you love someone, you will be loyal to him no matter what the cost. You will always believe in him, always expect the best of him, and always stand your ground in defending him.

1 CORINTHIANS 13:7 TLB

This is a call to believe the best in others. It's knowing they're not perfect, but purposeful in how they live. It's being a faithful friend and knowing when to speak hard truth laced with love. It's caring enough to challenge their wrong thinking, calling them higher when necessary. It's defending their name and being a steadfast champion as they walk through life's storms. Loving others is active.

This takes intentionality, because life is busy and sometimes overwhelming with responsibility. Being loyal to others is only born from a heart full of faith, a direct result of time spent with God. He is the one who will give us the desire and ability to offer dependable love to others.

DEAR LORD, FILL ME WITH LOVE FOR OTHERS THAT IS FAITHFUL AND RELIABLE. IN JESUS' NAME, AMEN.

The Investment of Love

All the special gifts and powers from God will someday come to an end, but love goes on forever.
1 CORINTHIANS 13:8 TLB

There is an ending for so many things here on earth. Eventually, even God's gifts like prophecy, speaking in tongues, and knowledge will be fulfilled, lose their value, and cease to exist. But scripture says love will never end. It will never fade out or become unimportant. It will never fail.

Knowing that, invest heavily in it. Look for ways to express compassion and kindness every day. Ask the Lord to open your eyes and stir your spirit. From feeding a stranger on the street, donating to a worthy charity, cleaning a friend's home while she's sick, or speaking encouragement to the weary, let love be a driving force. Look for ways to be God's hands and feet to a hurting world. Know that each time you show benevolence, the Lord takes notice. He is well pleased with your kindness.

DEAR LORD, HELP ME INVEST IN LOVING OTHERS! IN JESUS' NAME, AMEN.

The Greatest Is Love

But now faith, hope, and love remain; these three virtues must characterize our lives. The greatest of these is love.

1 CORINTHIANS 13:13 VOICE

At the center of God's character is love. This is foundational to the Christian life because loving God and others is the greatest command. From this, we can clearly understand the value the Lord puts on it. It's at the heart of everything.

But why is love more important than faith and hope? It's simply because without it, faith and hope cannot exist. Love is what fuels them. It makes walking them out possible for believers. So, if we aren't putting in the effort to deepen our love for God and others, we won't grow in our faith walk or experience genuine hope.

Daily time in the Word, a robust prayer life, and a community of believers will help love to mature into something beautiful that will help faith and hope come alive.

DEAR LORD, HELP ME LOVE YOU AND OTHERS WITH PURPOSE. IN JESUS' NAME, AMEN.

When Love Feels Thin

Be alert. Be firm in the Christian faith.
Be courageous and strong. Do everything with love.
1 CORINTHIANS 16:13–14 GW

For many, the first few commands in today's verses are doable. We can be attentive and prepared for what's ahead. We can be unashamed of the gospel and bold in our faith. We can even exhibit strength and confidence when the storms of life hit. But we get tripped up when instructed to do *everything* with love. Sometimes the reality of it just feels too big.

Every day, we should humbly ask God for the ability to love because it doesn't always come easily, especially toward those we find frustrating or selfish. We need His help since we tend to show kindness and compassion conditionally. It's only through God's help we can experience supernatural love that makes this command possible.

As you lean on the Lord when your ability to love feels thin, watch how He empowers you in extraordinary ways.

DEAR LORD, HELP ME LOVE THE UNLOVABLE. IN JESUS' NAME, AMEN.

Serving in Love

As for you, my friends, you were called to be free. But do not let this freedom become an excuse for letting your physical desires control you. Instead, let love make you serve one another.

GALATIANS 5:13 GNT

Paul reminds us that our freedom isn't a license to live however we want and to do whatever we want. It's not for selfish purposes. Instead, as we recognize the depth of God's love for us that sent His Son to the cross, it should drive us to live with a servant's heart. Our greatest desire should be to love the Lord and others in meaningful ways that reflect His love.

In what ways can you walk this out? How can you serve others with compassion and care? How can you use your freedom in Christ to be His hands and feet? How can you demonstrate your genuine love to those around you? Ask God to show you.

DEAR LORD, THANK YOU FOR MY FREEDOM! HELP ME USE IT TO SERVE IN LOVE. IN JESUS' NAME, AMEN.

Letting Your Love Shine

For the whole Law can be summed up in this one command: "Love others as you love yourself."
GALATIANS 5:14 TLB

Think about how you take care of yourself. You are careful to get enough rest. You try to eat a balanced diet (well. . .mostly) and exercise regularly. You treat yourself to what makes you happy. You keep your home nicely decorated and keep it clean. Maybe you splurge on hair and nails and cute clothes. For the most part, you are intentional in showing love to yourself.

God wants you to care that much for others. Rather than being self-focused, He expects you to treat others just as kindly. Offer to help. Bring a meal. Treat someone to a spa day. Take a walk with a friend. Listen when they share their heart. Give a gift in celebration. Point them to the Father. Let your love shine and let others know they matter.

DEAR LORD, HELP ME SHINE WITH LOVE AND TREAT OTHERS WITH CARE. IN JESUS' NAME, AMEN.

Sacrificial Love

"For God loved the world so much that he gave his only Son so that anyone who believes in him shall not perish but have eternal life."

JOHN 3:16 TLB

Now *that's* a demonstration of sacrificial love. You may care deeply for others and want the very best for them. Your heart may be extremely invested in friends and family. You may even think there are no limits to your compassion and devotion. But only God could love so lavishly that He willingly gave His only Son to bridge the gap that sin left.

We're called to love generously too. Would you make a meal for a sick neighbor or offer free babysitting? Would you give up a weekend to help a friend move? Would you support a charitable cause with your time, even if it is inconvenient?

God gave the ultimate sacrifice for you without a second thought. His love is undeniable. Would others say your love is undeniable too?

DEAR LORD, HELP ME LOVE WILLINGLY AND SACRIFICIALLY. IN JESUS' NAME, AMEN.

Practice Loving Others

Dear friends, let us practice loving each other, for love comes from God and those who are loving and kind show that they are the children of God, and that they are getting to know him better.

1 John 4:7 TLB

Scripture tells us to practice loving others. So how do we do that? Just as you would put in the time to become a good baker, writer, or artist, you must also learn to love well. It doesn't always come naturally. Everyone feels love differently. Some respond to words of affirmation, while others need quality time. Maybe they need a bear hug or a thoughtful gift. Or maybe they feel loved when you do something kind and helpful.

Become a student of those you care about. How do your parents feel appreciated? What makes your best friend feel important? How can you best express your deep feelings to your husband?

DEAR LORD, OPEN MY EYES TO SEE HOW OTHERS NEED TO FEEL LOVED THE BEST. IN JESUS' NAME, AMEN.

How could we turn our hearts away from someone who we deem unlovable when God chose to love us in our sin?

Loving Rightly

So, my loved ones, if God loved us so sacrificially, surely we should love one another.

1 JOHN 4:11 VOICE

There's no good excuse for us to not love others. As believers, how could we turn our hearts away from someone who we deem unlovable when God chose to love us *in our sin*? He didn't wait until we were less wretched. We didn't have to get cleaned up. Instead, the Lord showed extravagant love right where we were. So let us do the same.

This doesn't mean we stay in abusive relationships or let others walk all over us in the name of loving them. It's good and necessary to have healthy boundaries in place. Sometimes loving means we have tough conversations and let people walk out the consequences of their actions. But let's make sure our heart for them is good rather than bitter. Ask God to help you love rightly.

DEAR LORD, SHOW ME HOW TO LOVE IN THE RIGHT WAYS. IN JESUS' NAME, AMEN.

Love Over Hate

God showed how much he loved us by sending his only Son into this wicked world to bring to us eternal life through his death. In this act we see what real love is: it is not our love for God but his love for us when he sent his Son to satisfy God's anger against our sins.

1 JOHN 4:9–10 TLB

Jesus stepped out of heaven and into this wicked world simply because we mattered so deeply to Him. The thought of eternal separation from His creation was unacceptable, so God made an extraordinary decision that satisfied His anger.

Knowing that, how can we let our hearts become filled with hate? If the Lord didn't, how can we decide someone is unworthy of our kindness and generosity? How can we turn our backs on those we see as unlovable? Ask God to help you respond in love, appropriately, and with necessary limits when you feel incapable.

DEAR LORD, EMPOWER ME TO CHOOSE LOVE OVER HATE. IN JESUS' NAME, AMEN.

Proof God Lives in You

No one has ever seen God. If we love each other, God lives in us, and his love is perfected in us. We know that we live in him and he lives in us because he has given us his Spirit.

1 JOHN 4:12–13 GW

Today's scripture reminds us that treating others with love and respect proves that God's Holy Spirit lives in us. If we show genuine compassion with the right motives to those around us, His love is certainly being perfected in us. We should be encouraged each time our heart is tendered toward someone, whether they are hurting and hopeless or happy and healthy. That kind of love comes from God.

Time in His Word will bring about a change in how you think of others. You will notice a sensitivity to what they may be facing. There will be a desire to connect in meaningful ways as you deepen relationships.

DEAR LORD, THANK YOU THAT YOUR SPIRIT IN ME HELPS ME LOVE OTHERS WELL! IN JESUS' NAME, AMEN.

An Unquestionable Truth

We know how much God loves us because we have felt his love and because we believe him when he tells us that he loves us dearly. God is love, and anyone who lives in love is living with God and God is living in him.

1 JOHN 4:16 TLB

Do you believe that God loves you, friend? Sometimes it's difficult to understand how a perfect God can love very imperfect people. We may think He's disappointed in us or angry that we make mistakes. We may feel ashamed because we can't stop sinning in certain ways. Rather than run to the Lord when we mess up, we hide and stay silent, assuming we are beyond forgiveness. But that simply isn't true.

God wants you to *know* how much He loves you. Without any doubt, He wants it to be an unquestionable truth in your heart. Ask the Father to reveal this to you and then watch as He shows you just how much.

DEAR LORD, REVEAL YOUR LOVE
TO ME. IN JESUS' NAME, AMEN.

No Need to Fear

We need have no fear of someone who loves us perfectly; his perfect love for us eliminates all dread of what he might do to us. If we are afraid, it is for fear of what he might do to us and shows that we are not fully convinced that he really loves us.

1 John 4:18 TLB

There is no need to be afraid of God and His wrath. You don't need to worry about the proverbial lightning bolt striking you when you make mistakes. He won't step out of heaven to come down and scold you mercilessly. But because God loves you perfectly, He will convict you through the Holy Spirit. It's that gut feeling that's encouraging you to repent and make better choices.

If you're truly worried about what He might do if you upset Him, talk to God. Be honest. Read what the Word says about His love. Ask Him to help you accept His perfect love with confidence.

DEAR LORD, HELP ME TRUST YOUR LOVE. IN JESUS' NAME, AMEN.

Alignment

If anyone says "I love God," but keeps on hating his brother, he is a liar; for if he doesn't love his brother who is right there in front of him, how can he love God whom he has never seen? And God himself has said that one must love not only God but his brother too.

1 JOHN 4:20–21 TLB

As believers, our words and actions should align in many areas, but especially in how we love. Today's scripture echoes this by asking a powerful question: How can we hate someone and love God at the same time? We can't, which means we desperately need His help.

When you struggle to show care and compassion to others—even when it feels justified—ask the Lord to help you love them *through* Him. Confess your struggle, sharing the details of your heart. Ask God to replace your perspective and understanding with His so you can see that person as He does.

DEAR LORD, HELP MY LOVE FOR OTHERS ALIGN WITH YOURS. IN JESUS' NAME, AMEN.

Handling Offenses

Most of all, love each other steadily and unselfishly, because love makes up for many faults.

1 PETER 4:8 VOICE

The goal is for us to love so fiercely that we're able to overlook offenses regularly. We should want peace more than we want to be right. Rather than keep a scorecard of wrongs, we choose to forgive quickly. We choose to trust that their heart for us is good and know that our heart for them is good too. So, when something they do or say stings, we can choose to let it go because of our love for one another.

That doesn't mean, however, that we can't express our feelings or call someone out for bad behavior. But we do so with truth and love, looking for quick and complete restoration. We listen to their heart too, being humble and apologizing where needed. Relationships work best when we are focused on loving and commit to reconciling before too much time passes.

DEAR LORD, LET LOVE REIGN MOST IN MY RELATIONSHIPS. IN JESUS' NAME, AMEN.

Loving Through Hospitality

Show hospitality to each other without complaint. Use whatever gift you've received for the good of one another so that you can show yourselves to be good stewards of God's grace in all its varieties.

1 PETER 4:9–10 VOICE

This is a call to be hospitable to other believers, using our spiritual talents to benefit one another. It's to be done ungrudgingly and without complaining. This can be challenging!

It's easier to show kindness when we're well-rested and life is calm. When bills are paid, food is in the pantry, and gas is in the tank, loving others feels natural. But hospitality may be the last thing we feel equipped to offer when our world feels chaotic and uncertain.

This is why we need God to work through us. We need Him to equip us with love and compassion. Be quick to pray when you feel unable to walk out today's verses and let the Lord empower you through faith.

DEAR LORD, I NEED YOU TO HELP ME LOVE WELL. IN JESUS' NAME, AMEN.

Truthfulness

Don't tell lies to each other; it was your old life with all its wickedness that did that sort of thing; now it is dead and gone.
COLOSSIANS 3:9 TLB

When you love someone, you work toward building trust with one another. You do this by choosing to be honest and authentic about your plans, your thoughts, your hopes, your feelings, and the like. You tell the truth, even when it's difficult to do. When you must share hard things, you speak with kindness and truth.

Do you struggle with sincerity? Is it hard for you to be open and direct with others? Remember that as a believer, the Holy Spirit lives in you to mature your faith into something beautiful. Listen for His voice and prompting to be truthful in every interaction. Love enough to be honest. It may be challenging, but it's a choice that benefits relationships in beautiful ways.

DEAR LORD, I WANT TO SHOW LOVE TO OTHERS BY BEING TRUTHFUL WITH THEM. IN JESUS' NAME, AMEN.

What Matters

In this new life one's nationality or race or education or social position is unimportant; such things mean nothing. Whether a person has Christ is what matters, and he is equally available to all.

COLOSSIANS 3:11 TLB

Scripture tells us that what matters most in this world is having a personal relationship with Jesus. But the world's voice is loud, telling us differently. Regardless, we are called to love others enough that we eagerly share the gospel message that's available to everyone.

Let's not show favoritism based on the list above. Nationality, race, education, and popularity don't adequately measure one's worth in the Lord's eyes. To Him, these carry no weight. They shouldn't for us either. Instead, let's demonstrate brotherly love by sharing Jesus with everyone equally, hoping for them to secure eternity in heaven with a saving faith. Let's see everyone's value through God's priorities.

DEAR LORD, HELP ME KEEP YOUR PERSPECTIVE ON WHAT MATTERS AND LOVE OTHERS ENOUGH TO SHARE THE GOSPEL MESSAGE. IN JESUS' NAME, AMEN.

Clothe Yourself

Since you are all set apart by God, made holy and dearly loved, clothe yourselves with a holy way of life: compassion, kindness, humility, gentleness, and patience.

COLOSSIANS 3:12 VOICE

Everything changes once you invite Jesus into your heart as your personal Savior. In that moment, you are set apart and made holy. You're now in the family of faith and dearly loved by the one who created you! The Holy Spirit works to transform your life in beautiful and powerful ways.

Where your heart was hardened, you're now filled with compassion for others. There's a genuine desire to be kind rather than judgmental. Patience blooms as you grow deeper in your faith. Humility replaces pride, and there begins to be a gentle spirit about you. These changes bless you and benefit others. So, clothe yourself in a holy way of life so that all you do points to God in heaven.

DEAR LORD, TRANSFORM ME INTO A WOMAN WHO PURSUES A HOLY WAY OF LIFE IN ALL I DO. IN JESUS' NAME, AMEN.

Put Up with One Another

Put up with one another. Forgive. Pardon any offenses against one another, as the Lord has pardoned you, because you should act in kind.
COLOSSIANS 3:13 VOICE

Tolerance is one way we show others they are loved. We don't give up on them or throw in the towel on a relationship when they mess up. We don't keep score of their wrongdoings, constantly reminding them of where and how they've fallen short. Instead, we decide to accept them as they are—stumbles, fumbles, and all. Isn't that what we want too? We love without conditions. We extend grace even when they don't deserve it.

If our goal and purpose is to love, then choosing to *put up with one another* is a good start! Let's remember that no one is perfect, including ourselves. We all need the freedom to make mistakes from time to time and still be loved.

DEAR LORD, LET ME SHOW LOVE TOWARD OTHERS BY ACCEPTING THEIR IMPERFECTIONS AND FLAWS WITHOUT JUDGMENT. IN JESUS' NAME, AMEN.

We all need the freedom to make mistakes from time to time and still be loved.

Put On Love

But above all these, put on love! Love is the perfect tie to bind these together. Let your hearts fall under the rule of the Anointed's peace (the peace you were called to as one body), and be thankful.

Colossians 3:14–15 VOICE

More than anything else, we're to clothe ourselves with love. We're to lead with it every day and in every interaction. It's to be the lens through which we look at others. But have you ever wondered what this looks like, practically speaking?

You can put others first, seeing that their needs are met. Be quick to forgive an offense rather than hold on to it. Show patience and be gentle with others, for you may not know what they're struggling with. Be compassionate. Be present. Be thoughtful. Choose kindness whenever possible. When you stay connected to God and let His words sink into your heart, love will naturally flow from it.

DEAR LORD, CLOTHE ME IN LOVE SO I CAN BE YOUR HANDS AND FEET TO A HURTING WORLD. IN JESUS' NAME, AMEN.

Celebrate Others

There is no greater way to love than to give your life for your friends. You celebrate our friendship if you obey this command.

John 15:13–14 VOICE

These verses point to the powerful gift of sacrificial love. They demonstrate the importance of giving rather than taking. They challenge believers to stop being self-focused first. But we don't have to give our lives to prove our love. We can show it in meaningful ways every day.

Take the time to celebrate others, both when they succeed and when they fail despite their best efforts. Recognize the brokenhearted by offering much-needed encouragement. Generously give of yourself through time and treasure. Commit to praying for someone daily. Open your home, cook a meal, lend an ear, extend a hand, or help them navigate the details of a difficult situation. These should be common responses from believers because we're called to imitate Jesus, who loved sacrificially, even with His own life.

DEAR LORD, TEACH ME TO CELEBRATE OTHERS LIKE YOU DO. IN JESUS' NAME, AMEN.

Not of the World

If you were a product of the world order, then it would love you. But you are not a product of the world because I have taken you out of it, and it despises you for that very reason.

JOHN 15:19 VOICE

Simply put, it's okay if the world doesn't love you. If they are critical and hurtful, it's alright. They may reject you for not subscribing to their idea of right and wrong, but don't be discouraged. You may face disappointments because you don't fit in, so be ready. Friend, if the world mistreats you, it's because you are not of it. You're a Christ follower now, and that sets you apart.

Let your value come from being God's child. Find your worth in a godly community with like-minded individuals who subscribe to the truths in His Word. Know that you are perfectly loved by a perfect Father who is crazy about you, which is all that matters.

DEAR LORD, I WANT YOUR LOVE OVER ANYTHING THE WORLD CAN OFFER. IN JESUS' NAME, AMEN.

Loving Like God

So I give you a new command: Love each other deeply and fully. Remember the ways that I have loved you, and demonstrate your love for others in those same ways. Everyone will know you as My followers if you demonstrate your love to others.

JOHN 13:34–35 VOICE

Think about the ways God has loved you. Maybe He answered your prayers by restoring an important relationship. Maybe He opened all the right doors for your career at the right time. Maybe the Lord gave you the robust community you asked for or provided financially when you found yourself in a pickle. Or maybe He healed your broken heart in supernatural ways. Regardless, God loved you in the ways you needed it.

Let's love others the same way. Ask Him to open your eyes to see how you can demonstrate kindness and compassion to those around you. How can you express your heartfelt feelings while meeting their needs? How can you offer support or friendship?

DEAR LORD, LET ME LOVE LIKE YOU DO. IN JESUS' NAME, AMEN.

Love Overlooks

Hatred stirs old quarrels, but love overlooks insults.
PROVERBS 10:12 TLB

It's not easy to overlook the insults others throw in your direction or let mean-spirited words roll off your back. When your feelings get hurt, choosing quick forgiveness can be challenging. But when love is our passion and pursuit, and we find strength from God, we can do the impossible.

It's important to keep short accounts of wrongs. There's no good reason to tally up bad behavior. Our job is to love, and it's God's job to judge. We're to be kind and generous and leave conviction to the Lord. That doesn't mean we're a doormat to be walked on. We aren't meant to be a punching bag, taking verbal abuse quietly or regularly. We can (and should) set healthy boundaries so we stay safe. But when we are able to overlook insults and show love instead, we should.

DEAR LORD, WHEN INSULTS COME MY WAY, STRENGTHEN ME TO RESPOND IN LOVE RATHER THAN ANGER. IN JESUS' NAME, AMEN.

Imperfect Love

The most important commandment is this:
"Hear, O Israel, the Eternal One is our God, and the Eternal One is the only God. You should love the Eternal, your God, with all your heart, with all your soul, with all your mind, and with all your strength."

MARK 12:29–30 VOICE

Looking back at the command from today's verse, do you ever wonder just how can we love God in such ways? How can we love Him with *all* our heart, soul, mind, and strength, especially knowing our human limitations? Being flawed, is it truly possible to walk this out and meet His expectations?

What the Lord is looking for is purposefulness, not perfection. He created us, and He knows what we're capable of. He understands our inadequacies and where we're weak. But when we ask God to help us love Him better, we will find the strength. Time in the Word will direct our efforts. Pursuing righteousness keeps us focused.

DEAR LORD, HELP ME LOVE YOU BETTER. IN JESUS' NAME, AMEN.

Love in the Same Way

The second great commandment is this:
"Love others in the same way you love yourself."
MARK 12:31 VOICE

We can be so focused on taking care of our own needs that we are dismissive—sometimes innocently—of the needs of others. From a good night's sleep to a wardrobe refresh to healthy eating to time for self-care, we're often very protective of our own needs and wants. We don't stop to ask what others might need because we're too busy fulfilling our own desires.

There's nothing wrong with taking care of yourself. It's important. But let's make sure we are loving others at the same time and in the same ways. Let's keep our eyes open to their needs, showing them the same kindness and concern we show ourselves. As believers, we have the privilege and burden to love those around us with great intention.

DEAR LORD, I CONFESS THAT I SOMETIMES FOCUS SOLELY ON MY NEEDS AND NOT THE NEEDS OF OTHERS. HELP ME CHANGE THAT. IN JESUS' NAME, AMEN.

Loving Within Your Means

Then a poor widow came and dropped in two pennies. He called his disciples to him and remarked, "That poor widow has given more than all those rich men put together! For they gave a little of their extra fat, while she gave up her last penny."

MARK 12:42–44 TLB

Jesus recognized the poor widow's sacrificial gift of love, even though it was next to nothing on the world's scales. Her giving may have been modest to many, but her heart was rich with love. Let that encourage you today!

You don't have to overwhelm others with grand displays of love. You don't have to outdo or try to match the generosity of someone who has much more to offer. There's no standard you must strive to meet. Instead, you can show love within your means. You can express it through heartfelt encouragement, a cup of coffee, a small token of appreciation, or a modest gift.

DEAR LORD, LET ME BE CONFIDENT AS I LOVE WITHIN MY MEANS. IN JESUS' NAME, AMEN.

Let Love Motivate

If I gave everything I have to poor people, and if I were burned alive for preaching the Gospel but didn't love others, it would be of no value whatever.

1 CORINTHIANS 13:3 TLB

Loving others is of the utmost importance as believers. It's at the core of God's heart and a command to His followers. It's an expectation as we grow in our faith. It's also one of the most challenging things to do, because motive matters.

Scripture says that it's not our works alone that make a difference. Our actions may point to loving with abandon, but if our hearts aren't right, each show of compassion holds no value. Love should be what motivates us to be kind and generous. It should spill out and into how we treat those around us. It should prompt us to care. Love for others should provoke us to demonstrate it with a genuine, authentic desire.

DEAR LORD, LET ME BE KNOWN AS A WOMAN WHO IS MOTIVATED BY UNDISPUTABLE LOVE. IN JESUS' NAME, AMEN.

As We Were

But God has shown us how much he loves us—
it was while we were still sinners that Christ died for us!
Romans 5:8 GNT

We didn't have to get cleaned up for God to see our value. He wasn't waiting, looking for perfection from imperfect people. We weren't required to try and fix our sin issues to be more presentable. Instead, the Lord took the first step toward us, offering a way to bridge the gap caused by our human condition. While we were still drowning in our wretchedness and unable to save ourselves, God sent His Son to pay the price.

What a miraculous gift of mercy! What an unimaginable act of love! It was the Lord's relentless compassion for humanity that created the path forward for us to not only be in a right relationship with Him but also to be secure in our eternity in heaven. Let the depth of God's love for you seep deep into your heart.

DEAR LORD, THANK YOU FOR YOUR RELENTLESS LOVE. IN JESUS' NAME, AMEN.

You may not be able to love God perfectly, but you can choose to love Him with determination.

Showing God Your Love

Jesus answered, "'Love the Lord your God with all your heart, with all your soul, and with all your mind.' This is the greatest and the most important commandment."

MATTHEW 22:37–38 GNT

Every time you open your Bible, it shows God that you love Him. When you intentionally meditate on key scripture throughout the day, talk to the Lord, and share your thoughts, it blesses Him. When you are honest in prayer and committed to it, He feels your devotion. Telling others about God's goodness and encouraging them in the faith reveals your passion. And when you pursue righteous living, honoring Him in words and actions, He is delighted.

You may not be able to love God perfectly, but you can choose to love Him with determination. You can ask the Lord to help you walk this out each day with perseverance. You can open your heart to follow His leading. Let God help you love Him in meaningful ways.

DEAR LORD, SHOW ME HOW TO LOVE YOU BEST. IN JESUS' NAME, AMEN.

The Pursuit of Peace

Be always humble, gentle, and patient. Show your love by being tolerant with one another. Do your best to preserve the unity which the Spirit gives by means of the peace that binds you together.

EPHESIANS 4:2–3 GNT

A quick temper never conveys genuine love to anyone. When we're intolerant and critical, it doesn't create a warm and fuzzy feeling in the hearts of others. Neither does causing dissent where unity once stood. And when we act arrogant, abrasive, or annoyed, it's almost impossible for love to break through that tough exterior. Instead, God wants us to love those around us—our community—so each person experiences a feeling of acceptance that fosters togetherness. He wants us to live in peace and protect it with purpose.

What are some things that need to change so you can live this way? Where do you need God to strengthen your resolve? How can you become an agent of peace?

DEAR LORD, TEACH ME TO LOVE OTHERS THROUGH THE PURSUIT OF PEACE. IN JESUS' NAME, AMEN.

Truth Spoken in Love

Instead, by truth spoken in love, we are to grow in every way into Him—the Anointed One, the head. He joins and holds together the whole body with its ligaments providing the support needed so each part works to its proper design to form a healthy, growing, and mature body that builds itself up in love.

Ephesians 4:15–16 voice

To mature in our faith, it's essential we all work together. Community is important to our personal and collective development as believers. As we each do our part—using our God-given gifts to walk out the calling He's placed on our lives—we grow. Speaking the truth in love is the glue that holds us together.

Today's verses are talking about church unity and the need to teach each other truths about who God is and what He wants from His followers. We're to make certain new believers especially don't misunderstand the gospel truth found in the Word. Our motivation should always be love.

DEAR LORD, LET ME SPEAK TRUTH MOTIVATED BY LOVE. IN JESUS' NAME, AMEN.

Seeking Resolution

When you are angry, don't let it carry you into sin. Don't let the sun set with anger in your heart or give the devil room to work.

EPHESIANS 4:26–27 VOICE

No matter what relationship is causing you anger and frustration, today's verses apply. This is a call for thorough forgiveness. It's a challenge to keep short accounts of wrongs. Rather than carry a grudge, we're to seek resolution so the enemy has no room to work.

Is this easy to do? Not always. There are circumstances where the hurt feels too big to work out so quickly. You may need time to work things through as revelation keeps coming. But ask God to keep your heart tender and loving, with a desire to find solutions and answers. Ask Him to keep you from bitterness or a desire to get revenge. You can trust the Lord with your heartache. Let His love bring comfort and peace.

DEAR LORD, GIVE ME A HEART FOR RESOLUTION SO MY ABILITY TO LOVE ISN'T COMPROMISED. IN JESUS' NAME, AMEN.

Words Matter

Don't let even one rotten word seep out of your mouths.
Instead, offer only fresh words that build others up
when they need it most. That way your good words
will communicate grace to those who hear them.
EPHESIANS 4:29 VOICE

Yes, friend, our words matter! The fresh ones and the rotten ones hold great power. Used well, they can bring much-needed encouragement and usher in hope. Used recklessly, they will cut someone to the core and cause despair. It's up to us to choose them wisely. Sometimes, the best plan is to stay quiet and ask God to keep our mouths shut.

One of the five love languages is words of affirmation. When this is at the top of someone's list, speaking with kindness and love makes all the difference in the world. It fills their love bucket, strengthens their confidence, and makes them feel known and seen. Be careful with your words.

DEAR LORD, HELP ME BE DISCERNING
WITH MY WORDS SO OTHERS FEEL
LOVED. IN JESUS' NAME, AMEN.

Those Bad Days

Stop being mean, bad-tempered, and angry. Quarreling, harsh words, and dislike of others should have no place in your lives. Instead, be kind to each other, tenderhearted, forgiving one another, just as God has forgiven you because you belong to Christ.

Ephesians 4:31–32 TLB

The truth is that everyone has a bad day where we snap at people and treat those we love recklessly. We're human and we make mistakes. Be quick to apologize and try to let those bad days be few and far between.

If our goal is to love—albeit imperfectly—we should make every effort to treat others with kindness. We should be ready and willing to extend grace. Our words should be encouraging and our actions thoughtful. If we ask God to help us be compassionate and gentle, He will empower us to be so. It may not always be easy, but we can choose to live and love well.

DEAR LORD, WHEN THOSE BAD DAYS COME, GIVE ME THE STRENGTH TO CHOOSE KINDNESS. IN JESUS' NAME, AMEN.

The Spirit Empowers

"If you love me, you will obey my commandments. I will ask the Father, and he will give you another Helper, who will stay with you forever."

JOHN 14:15–16 GNT

One of the greatest gifts we've been given as believers is the presence of the Holy Spirit in our lives. He sparks our faith into action and patiently tends to the maturation of it. We cannot cause Him to leave us, nor can we send Him away. The Spirit is with us forever and empowers us to obey the Father's commands, which sends a huge message to Him. It reveals our love.

Remember that every time you do as He asks, it matters. God sees your obedience as a sign of love. It demonstrates your devotion. Choosing His way over your way speaks volumes and shows your allegiance. It's the Holy Spirit who gives you the prompting and power to obey.

DEAR LORD, THANK YOU FOR THE SPIRIT WHO WILL PROMPT ME TO OBEY AND GIVE ME THE POWER TO DO SO. IN JESUS' NAME, AMEN.

Why We Need His Peace

"I am leaving you with a gift—peace of mind and heart! And the peace I give isn't fragile like the peace the world gives. So don't be troubled or afraid."

JOHN 14:27 TLB

The peace of Jesus is unmatched by anything the world can offer. It's better than any self-help book, comfort food, retail therapy, or girlfriend time. While these things may be nice, what they provide is often fragile and short-lived. Even a swanky spa getaway or secluded beach vacation can't offer the long-term peace that Jesus provides to believers.

One of the reasons we need to pursue His peace above all else is because it will help us find the ability to love others well. When our heart is calm and our spirit is settled, we can be intentional and present with those we care about. We can show compassion with purpose, and we can be a blessing in wonderful ways.

DEAR LORD, WHEN I LOOK TO THE WORLD FOR PEACE, REMIND ME YOURS IS ALL I NEED. IN JESUS' NAME, AMEN.

Showing Love

Friends always show their love.
What are relatives for if not to share trouble?
PROVERBS 17:17 GNT

What are the ways you show love? Maybe you are a confidante who helps a friend navigate a tough marriage. Maybe you are the one who organizes get-togethers, making sure your friend group connects regularly. Maybe you are the caretaker for aging parents or volunteer your time in the community. Maybe you love to bake, and your neighbors are the recipients of your goodies. Or maybe you help someone with childcare, carpooling, or tutoring.

God is delighted when we prioritize kindness. It pleases Him to see us pour time and effort into the lives of others. And when we obey His command to love others in the ways that matter most to them, the Lord smiles down from heaven. Let's be women who seize opportunities to show care and generosity to those around us. Let's keep our eyes and ears open so we can bless others.

DEAR LORD, LET ME BE DEMONSTRATIVE IN SHOWING LOVE. IN JESUS' NAME, AMEN.

You're in the Family

See how very much our heavenly Father loves us,
for he allows us to be called his children—think of it—
and we really are! But since most people don't know God,
naturally they don't understand that we are his children.

1 JOHN 3:1 TLB

It's both an honor and a privilege to be called God's daughter. Think about it. The one who spoke this world into existence. The one who made the world and everything in it. The one who is over everything and everyone—both heavenly and earthly. The one who is all-powerful and all-knowing is your *Father*.

It's His unfailing love that allows you 24/7/365 access to Him. You can cry out at any time. You can lay every fear and worry at His feet as they creep in. You can share your challenges and celebrations in detail, whether it's noon or midnight. You are so very loved that God chose to bring you in the family—now and forever.

DEAR LORD, THANK YOU FOR BEING MY HEAVENLY FATHER! IN JESUS' NAME, AMEN.

What Love Reveals

So now we can tell who is a child of God and who belongs to Satan. Whoever is living a life of sin and doesn't love his brother shows that he is not in God's family; for the message to us from the beginning has been that we should love one another.

1 JOHN 3:10–11 TLB

When love is not evident, when someone doesn't show compassion and care toward others and instead embraces a sinful life—according to scripture—they are not in Christ. To the Lord, love is of the utmost importance.

Our belief in God should create in us a desire to express kindness and generosity with our time and treasure. Our hearts should be tendered to the point of benevolence. And because He first loved us, we should want to share that love in significant and meaningful ways with others.

DEAR LORD, BECAUSE I AM IN YOUR FAMILY, LET ME SHOW LOVE EXTRAVAGANTLY. IN JESUS' NAME, AMEN.

Spreading Goodwill in the World

So do not be surprised, my friends, if the people of the world hate you. We know that we have left death and come over into life; we know it because we love others. Those who do not love are still under the power of death.

1 JOHN 3:13–14 GNT

This is a stark contrast between believers and nonbelievers. Love is the defining factor between the two. When you bring a meal to a sick friend, pay a utility bill for someone in financial stress, or spend the weekend helping your sister move, you're loving well. Every time you choose to be inconvenienced for the needs of others, it's because of compassion and care. These things happen because of Jesus in you.

Be the kind of woman who shares God's love with the world through your words and actions. If your kindness aggravates another, today's verse explains why. Don't let that stop you from spreading goodwill in the world.

DEAR LORD, I WILL LOVE OTHERS, NO MATTER WHAT. IN JESUS' NAME, AMEN.

Be the kind of woman
who shares God's love
with the world through
your words and actions.

Showing Love Through Financial Support

But if someone who is supposed to be a Christian has money enough to live well, and sees a brother in need, and won't help him—how can God's love be within him?

1 JOHN 3:17 TLB

One of the ways we can show our love toward others is by being willing to help them financially when times are tough. If we have the means to offer support—either big or small—we should. If we're listening and watching, we will recognize the Holy Spirit's prompting to step in with love.

We can trust that God loves us enough to know our own tangible needs. He understands the sacrifices we may make when coming to the aid of others. As you prayerfully consider stepping in with financial support, you can trust Him to take care of you too. Be careful not to be so concerned with your level of comfort that you don't care about theirs.

DEAR LORD, I TRUST YOU TO CARE FOR ME AS I CARE FOR OTHERS. IN JESUS' NAME, AMEN.

Aligning Words and Actions

Dear children, we must show love through actions that are sincere, not through empty words. This is how we will know that we belong to the truth and how we will be reassured in his presence.

1 JOHN 3:18–19 GW

It's easy to utter the words, "I love you." We whisper it to our loved ones at night or say it as we walk out the door in the morning. We end each coffee date with a hug and this powerful phrase. We write it in letters and text it daily. Saying *I love you* is an integral part of our day. But do we truly show it?

Today's verse is a timely reminder to make sure our words and actions line up. Are we backing up what we say with what we do? Is there a discrepancy between the two? Scripture says that when both align—although imperfectly at times—it will reveal that we are true believers.

DEAR LORD, I WANT TO LOVE OTHERS CONSISTENTLY WITH BOTH MY WORDS AND ACTIONS. IN JESUS' NAME, AMEN.

The Debt of Love

Pay all your debts except the debt of love for others—never finish paying that! For if you love them, you will be obeying all of God's laws, fulfilling all his requirements.

Romans 13:8 TLB

We should never come to the end of our efforts to love someone. There isn't an end date to work toward. Instead, love is a "debt" that can't ever be paid off. We should show others—with perseverance and intentionality—how much they mean to us every day. Not only will that bless them and fill us with satisfaction, but it will also demonstrate our obedience to God. His command is that we love others with passion and purpose.

How are you doing with this directive? How are you showing compassion and consideration to others? How well are you filling the love buckets of those around you? In your opinion, have you paid your debt, or is loving others something you work toward every day?

DEAR LORD, LET THE DEBT OF LOVE NEVER BE PAID. IN JESUS' NAME, AMEN.

Love Is Never Harmful

Love never does anything that is harmful to a neighbor. Therefore, love fulfills Moses' Teachings.

ROMANS 13:10 GW

Love never does anything harmful. It doesn't treat others with contempt or look down on anyone in judgment. It's careful with words, making certain nothing is said in anger or in hurt that may be damaging to another's heart. Love doesn't manifest in reckless or risky ways. It's not toxic. It's not demanding. Love is never destructive in demonstration.

Maybe you grew up in a home where love was harmful, or maybe you've been in a relationship that deeply wounded you. Take every bit of this pain to God in prayer, be it daily, weekly, or hourly. Ask Him to heal your tangled heart and teach you to love others well. Just because love has been dysfunctional in your past doesn't mean it has to be that way in your future.

DEAR LORD, I DON'T WANT TO LOVE OTHERS IN THE HARMFUL WAYS I'VE EXPERIENCED. HEAL ME AND HELP ME LOVE ACCORDING TO YOUR WILL. IN JESUS' NAME, AMEN.

Loving the Unlovable

Don't just pretend that you love others: really love them. Hate what is wrong. Stand on the side of the good. Love each other with brotherly affection and take delight in honoring each other.

ROMANS 12:9–10 TLB

Today's verses are a challenge to not just act like we care about others but to let it be genuine. This is a call to respond kindly and authentically and to be selfless toward those around us. Honestly, sometimes walking this out toward everyone we meet feels almost impossible.

The reality is that it's easy to love the lovable. They make it effortless to express true compassion and care. We find joy in being around them. The tension comes when we try to love the unlovable. They get on our last nerve for a number of reasons. Only God can pave the path forward so we can take delight in and honor them. Ask for His help, trusting He will empower you.

DEAR LORD, I CAN'T LOVE WELL WITHOUT YOUR HELP. GIVE ME THE STRENGTH! IN JESUS' NAME, AMEN.

Opening Heart and Home

When God's children are in need, you be the one to help them out. And get into the habit of inviting guests home for dinner or, if they need lodging, for the night.

ROMANS 12:13 TLB

Hospitality is one way we can show love to others. You may feel like your home is your sanctuary, but opening it up and inviting people in speaks volumes. If you enjoy cooking, share a meal with friends and family. Fill their bellies with good food as you fellowship together. If someone needs a place to stay—either long- or short-term—be willing to discuss that as a viable option. If there's a way you're able to meet a need, prayerfully consider it and respond to God's prompting.

Loving others can sometimes mean we're inconvenienced and stretched. But when you involve the Lord and commit to following His lead, you'll be equipped to love in all the right ways.

DEAR LORD, EMPOWER ME TO OPEN MY HEART AND HOME ACCORDING TO YOUR WILL. IN JESUS' NAME, AMEN.

Always Speak Blessings

If people mistreat or malign you, bless them.
Always speak blessings, not curses.
ROMANS 12:14 VOICE

Sometimes what God asks seems impossible to walk out. For some, today's verse may feel this way. We are called to *always* speak blessings. Not some of the time. Not just when it's easy. And not just when we're well-rested and calm. The Lord expects believers to tame their tongues and *always* speak blessings, even when there are good reasons to do the opposite.

While we recognize our humanity and know we're terribly flawed, the idea here is to be mindful. It's about growing that self-control muscle and making the right choices. It's about responding in the spirit and not the flesh. When we ask God for strength and compassion to speak blessings and not curses, He will enable us to do the right thing. Loving others with our words is both a tall challenge and a command.

DEAR LORD, LET ME BE A WOMAN WHO IS ALWAYS CAREFUL WITH WORDS. IN JESUS' NAME, AMEN.

Loving People with Your Presence

If some have cause to celebrate, join in the celebration.
And if others are weeping, join in that as well.
ROMANS 12:15 VOICE

This is called the ministry of presence, and it's a powerful way to express love to those around you. This requires us to see and know what's happening in the lives of those we care about. We need to stay connected to know their joys and challenges. It means we know when to set aside our needs, our schedules, and our desires to be present with our friends and family.

When there is a reason to celebrate someone, make sure to be there. Cheer them on! Speak encouragement or congratulations. Likewise, be sure to show up when someone is struggling. Pray for them. Sit with them. Offer your support however they need it, or just act in kind ways without their prompting. Love people with your presence.

DEAR LORD, HELP ME KNOW WHEN AND HOW TO RESPOND TO OTHERS IN THE RIGHT WAYS AND AT THE RIGHT TIMES. IN JESUS' NAME, AMEN.

Appreciating the Differences in Others

Work toward unity, and live in harmony with one another. Avoid thinking you are better than others or wiser than the rest; instead, embrace common people and ordinary tasks.

Romans 12:16 voice

Nothing good comes from thinking you're better than someone else. Assuming you're smarter, more thoughtful, kinder, or wiser only works to separate you. It may be true in some situations, but elevating yourself doesn't take into consideration that we all have different strengths and challenges. Where you shine in one area, others may shine in another. The goal is to celebrate the ways God has made us unique. That's how you love with purpose.

What is the Holy Spirit speaking to you right now? Are there places you need to level the playing field in your mind and heart toward others? Do you need to repent? Let's choose to love without ranking one another. Doing so will usher in unity.

DEAR LORD, I CONFESS THE TIMES I'VE THOUGHT MYSELF BETTER THAN OTHERS. HELP ME APPRECIATE DIFFERENCES MOVING FORWARD. IN JESUS' NAME, AMEN.

God Will Handle It

Dear friends, never avenge yourselves. Leave that to God, for he has said that he will repay those who deserve it. Don't take the law into your own hands. Instead, feed your enemy if he is hungry. If he is thirsty give him something to drink and you will be "heaping coals of fire on his head." In other words, he will feel ashamed of himself for what he has done to you.

Romans 12:19–20 TLB

Rather than letting anger take root and bitterness set in, believers are to choose love. God has seen all that's taken place. He knows the ins and outs of the situation. He understands every detail completely and He promises to handle it on our behalf. He'll be the one to make right what was wrong. This frees us up to show kindness and compassion, something God will empower us to do as we lean on Him for help.

DEAR LORD, IT'S HARD TO LOVE THOSE WHO HURT ME. GIVE ME THE STRENGTH TO DO SO. IN JESUS' NAME, AMEN.

Trust Him to work
all things out for your
good and His glory.

Showing Love Through Restraint

Don't pay people back with evil for the evil they do to you.
Focus your thoughts on those things that are considered noble.
As much as it is possible, live in peace with everyone.
ROMANS 12:17–18 GW

The mandate is clear. We're to do our very best to live peacefully with those around us. When someone tries to pick a fight, we don't engage. When they say mean-spirited things, we choose the high road. When they try to take advantage of us, we advocate for ourselves firmly but kindly. And when we see an open door for payback, we don't walk through it. Instead, we show love through restraint.

Ask God to tender your heart and open your eyes to see what's really going on with the person trying to hurt you. Let Him settle your spirit. Let God bring comfort and peace. Then trust Him to work all things out for your good and His glory.

DEAR LORD, LET ME LIVE IN PEACE
WITH OTHERS AS MUCH AS POSSIBLE.
IN JESUS' NAME, AMEN.

Loving Begins with Prayer

"Listen, all of you. Love your enemies. Do good to those who hate you. Pray for the happiness of those who curse you; implore God's blessing on those who hurt you."

LUKE 6:27–28 TLB

Let this mandate sink in and challenge you to love hard because that's what walking this out will entail. We can love those who are kind, but this is next level love that requires God's help. And that's okay!

Just like everything else, the first step to loving your enemies begins with prayer. It's an opportunity to humble ourselves before the Father and ask for help. It's where we find the compassion to pray for those who've hurt us. Without that time with God to get our hearts right, it would be difficult to genuinely pray blessings on them. Without His supernatural empowerment, our faith will falter when those challenging moments come. We simply cannot love without the Lord's strength.

DEAR LORD, REMIND ME THAT MY ABILITY TO LOVE COMES FROM YOU. IN JESUS' NAME, AMEN.

How to Treat Others

"Give what you have to anyone who asks you for it; and when things are taken away from you, don't worry about getting them back. Treat others as you want them to treat you."

LUKE 6:30–31 TLB

When Jesus told us the second greatest command was to love our neighbors as ourselves, He meant it. That mandate is mentioned throughout the Bible in different forms but with the same sentiment. Today's verses echo that truth with clarity.

We're to treat others like we want to be treated, not as they deserve to be treated. There's a big difference. We show them love through compassion, ensuring their tangible needs are met. We show concern for their mental and emotional health by checking in with them regularly. Whenever possible, we're selfless with our time and treasure to be God's hands and feet. Because honestly, this is how we want to be loved by those around us.

DEAR LORD, HELP ME LOVE OTHERS IN THE WAYS I WANT TO BE LOVED BACK. IN JESUS' NAME, AMEN.

Imitating God's Love

So imitate God and be truly compassionate,
the way your Father is. If you don't want to be judged,
don't judge. If you don't want to be condemned,
don't condemn. If you want to be forgiven, forgive.
LUKE 6:36–37 VOICE

The Lord is the best, most perfect role model we could ever follow. Better than any celebrity or politician. Better than any pastor or small group leader. If we imitate God's love, those around us will be deeply blessed. We certainly can't duplicate His divinity or replicate His righteousness, but we can intentionally and purposefully show kindness in meaningful ways that matter.

Who are your role models, friend? Who are the people you hold up as examples of how to live and love well? If it's anyone other than the Lord, respectfully, it's time to aim higher. Read the Bible, spend time in prayer, and let His words lead your heart as you interact with others.

DEAR LORD, TEACH ME TO IMITATE
YOUR LOVE. IN JESUS' NAME, AMEN.

Giving to Others

"Give to others, and God will give to you.
Indeed, you will receive a full measure,
a generous helping, poured into your hands—
all that you can hold. The measure you use for
others is the one that God will use for you."
Luke 6:38 GNT

Today's verse is a call to generosity. It's a reminder that God sees the choices we make. It challenges us to lavish love onto those around us, not only because we want the Lord to give back to us but because we want others to feel seen and known. We want them to feel wanted and valued. And we know the power of feeling like we belong.

Friend, be bold in how you bless people, whether it's your neighbor, sister, father, coworker, or a stranger on the street. Be generous with your resources, trusting God will replenish as needed and according to His will. Be tenderhearted and love others with enthusiasm.

DEAR LORD, LET ME BE GENEROUS
TO THOSE YOU PLACE IN MY PATH.
IN JESUS' NAME, AMEN.

From the Heart

"A good person brings good out of the treasure of good things in his heart; a bad person brings bad out of his treasure of bad things. For the mouth speaks what the heart is full of."

Luke 6:45 GNT

How can we fill our hearts with good things so goodness is revealed in our words and actions? The best and most reliable way is to spend time in God's Word, to let it transform us from the inside out, and to put into action what it says.

When it tells us to forgive, we forgive quickly and fully. When it tells us to love, we love with passion and purpose. When it tells us to keep our eyes on the sacred and not the secular, we make wise choices. And when we pay attention to what goes into our minds, others will be blessed by what comes out of our hearts.

DEAR LORD, HELP ME FOCUS ON STORING GOOD THINGS IN MY HEART SO LOVE FLOWS FROM IT TOWARD OTHERS. IN JESUS' NAME, AMEN.

God's Love Is Stable

For I am convinced that nothing can ever separate us from his love. Death can't, and life can't. The angels won't, and all the powers of hell itself cannot keep God's love away. Our fears for today, our worries about tomorrow, or where we are—high above the sky, or in the deepest ocean—nothing will ever be able to separate us from the love of God demonstrated by our Lord Jesus Christ when he died for us.

ROMANS 8:38–39 TLB

There is great comfort for believers in knowing God's love is stable. There is nothing we can do to make Him love us any more or less than He does right now. Our seasons of sinning and bad choices cannot separate us. Our pursuit of righteousness doesn't garner more love from God.

At this very moment, we are fully and completely loved, and that truth is unchangeable by anything or anyone. Let that reality bless your heart today and always.

DEAR LORD, THANK YOU FOR YOUR STABLE LOVE. IN JESUS' NAME, AMEN.

Empowered to Live and Love Well

So be careful how you live; be mindful of your steps.
Don't run around like idiots as the rest of the world does.
Instead, walk as the wise! Make the most of every living
and breathing moment because these are evil times.
EPHESIANS 5:15–16 VOICE

The call to be careful in how we live and seek godly wisdom is essential for believers. To live with joy and perseverance, squeezing the goodness out of every moment is a blessing. When we're living correctly, our ability to love others with tenacity will be a natural outflow.

As believers, our ability to pursue holiness requires a meaningful connection with God. Our faith is fueled through His Spirit. As we invest in a relationship with Him, we'll be empowered to live well and love others the way the Lord commands. Let's be women who embrace righteousness in every way we can.

DEAR LORD, EMPOWER ME TO LIVE CAREFULLY AND KINDLY, MAKING THE MOST OF EVERY MOMENT WITH OTHERS. IN JESUS' NAME, AMEN.

Loyal Love

I want you to know that the Eternal your God is the only true God. He's the faithful God who keeps His covenants and shows loyal love for a thousand generations to those who in return love Him and keep His commands.

DEUTERONOMY 7:9 VOICE

God never loses His love for us. Once a promise is made, that promise is kept in every way. Even when people have let Him down, rejecting His commands, following temptation without care, and being filled with anger toward Him, God's heart has never changed. It never will. His love is loyal forever. Imagine that!

If we seek the Lord's help, we can also be loyal in our care for others. It won't be perfect or consistent—our human condition will make sure of that—but our love for those around us can be focused and firm, nonetheless. We can be faithful, imitating God's example of steadfast love as best as possible.

DEAR LORD, EMPOWER ME TO LOVE OTHERS FAITHFULLY. THANK YOU FOR SETTING THE EXAMPLE. IN JESUS' NAME, AMEN.

God Celebrates You

The Eternal your God is standing right here among you, and He is the champion who will rescue you. He will joyfully celebrate over you; He will rest in His love for you; He will joyfully sing because of you like a new husband.

ZEPHANIAH 3:17 VOICE

In this verse, Zephaniah talks about a time when God's judgment of Israel is complete, and Jesus will reign with His people in the millennial kingdom in Jerusalem. But doesn't this verse also paint a powerful image for every believer?

God may be celebrating over Jerusalem, but He also celebrates over you, friend. He is joyful about His beloved daughter! The Lord's love for you is secure, and He sings jubilantly because of it. Life may be hard now, but rest knowing how crazy the Father is about you. You can find comfort in the fact that a new world is coming without pain or tears.

DEAR LORD, HOLD ME CLOSE TODAY SO I FEEL YOUR LOVE AND HOPE. IN JESUS' NAME, AMEN.

Trust God More

Never tire of loyalty and kindness. Hold these virtues tightly. Write them deep within your heart. If you want favor with both God and man, and a reputation for good judgment and common sense, then trust the Lord completely; don't ever trust yourself.

PROVERBS 3:3–5 TLB

If you lean on yourself for the ability to live a life of goodness, you'll fall short every time. Trusting only your own wisdom and strength will lead to disappointment. And trying to love others with devotion and acting in kindness without God's help is foolish.

We need the Lord's power to be who He created us to be. Our desires may be in the right places, but our hearts are deceitful, and we have natural limitations to confront. So, let's choose to trust God completely. We'll love others better when we lean on Him for what we need.

DEAR LORD, I NEED YOUR STRENGTH OVER MINE SO I CAN BE A BLESSING TO OTHERS. IN JESUS' NAME, AMEN.

When God Corrects

My child, when the LORD corrects you, pay close attention and take it as a warning. The LORD corrects those he loves, as parents correct a child of whom they are proud.

PROVERBS 3:11–12 GNT

It may seem (and feel) counterintuitive, but when God brings correction, recognize it as something good. Scripture tells us that just like any thoughtful parent, God's correction is an act of genuine love. If God didn't care, He'd leave you alone to continue down destructive pathways. This correction also confirms that you are His beloved child and part of His family.

Change your view of God's discipline and let it bring a sweet affirmation to your spirit. You are deeply and completely loved by your heavenly Father, who cares enough to keep you headed in the right direction. What a blessing to know God will step in at the right time and in the right ways to protect you. Yes, you matter that much.

DEAR LORD, I KNOW YOU CORRECT ME BECAUSE YOU LOVE ME. IN JESUS' NAME, AMEN.

You are. . .loved by your heavenly Father, who cares enough to keep you headed in the right direction.

Putting Love into Action

Do not send your neighbor away, saying,
"Get back with me tomorrow. I can give it to you then,"
when what he needs is already in your hand. Make no
plans that could result in injury to your neighbor; after all,
he should be more secure because he lives near you.
PROVERBS 3:28–29 VOICE

Love in action is a powerful thing. While there may be times to postpone or wait to act, don't let that be your default response. If there is something you can do today to support a friend, do it. Be ready to help a family member at a moment's notice. When your neighbors reach out for assistance, clear your calendar and serve them. There are times when the kindest thing we can do is put love into action immediately.

Can you remember when someone came to your aid right when you needed it? Choose to be the kind of woman who offers love in motion when necessary.

DEAR LORD, I WILL PUT LOVE INTO ACTION. IN JESUS' NAME, AMEN.

Choosing Love as a Response

Whoever forgives an offense seeks love, but whoever keeps bringing up the issue separates the closest of friends.

PROVERBS 17:9 GW

Can you think of those who have offended you in the past? Chances are it's a lengthy list of names. From a parent who belittled you, to a boss who showed favoritism to your coworker, to a friend who let you down, to a husband who betrayed your trust, we have all been deeply hurt. It's how you respond to those painful moments that matters.

God wants us to choose love as a response instead of trying to smear their name. He wants us to forgive rather than look to exact revenge. We can respectfully confront, advocate for ourselves, and create healthy boundaries, but the driving force for our interactions should be following God's command to love. We should show restraint on our end, trusting the Lord to manage the situation with His justice.

DEAR LORD, HELP ME RESPOND IN LOVE TO THOSE WHO HURT ME INSTEAD OF CAUSING DIVISION. IN JESUS' NAME, AMEN.

Growing the Fruit

The Holy Spirit produces a different kind of fruit:
unconditional love, joy, peace, patience, kindheartedness,
goodness, faithfulness, gentleness, and self-control.
You won't find any law opposed to fruit like this.
GALATIANS 5:22–23 VOICE

The Holy Spirit plays a crucial role in the growth of a believer. Without Him, we'd run dangerously low on the fruit that every life of a Christ follower should produce. The truth is that we can't give others what we don't have. If the Spirit wasn't focused on maturing our faith—producing things like love, joy, kindness, and self-control—our ability to live well and show compassion would fall flat. We need His help to be a blessing to those around us.

Which fruit of the Spirit needs a shot of fertilizer? Where are you struggling to surrender yourself to the growth process? Let the Lord transform you from the inside out so you can be a positive influence and gift to the world.

DEAR LORD, LET MY LIFE REVEAL YOUR
INFLUENCE AND TRANSFORMATION.
IN JESUS' NAME, AMEN.

Better to Stay Humble

If we are living now by the Holy Spirit's power, let us follow the Holy Spirit's leading in every part of our lives. Then we won't need to look for honors and popularity, which lead to jealousy and hard feelings.

GALATIANS 5:25–26 TLB

Letting the Holy Spirit lead helps us take our eyes off the secular and instead focus on the sacred. We begin to care more about living a righteous life and being a source of joy to those we love. Rather than strive for status or push for popularity, we stay humble. We don't need to be better than anyone else. Instead, we look for ways to celebrate the wins and efforts of others.

The last thing we want is to be part of jealousy or hard feelings. It is better to avoid experiencing them or causing them. The Holy Spirit is trustworthy in ensuring we walk in ways that create unity and harmony, thereby loving others as God commands.

DEAR LORD, HELP ME SEEK HUMILITY OVER HONORS. IN JESUS' NAME, AMEN.

Working Toward Something Good

We are confident that God is able to orchestrate everything to work toward something good and beautiful when we love Him and accept His invitation to live according to His plan.

Romans 8:28 voice

In a display of God's great love, He makes a bold promise that should bolster our confidence in His goodness. No matter what life brings—heartache or challenges—He will work the details to bring blessings. It's a vow to produce beauty from our struggles.

Maybe you're battling a financial matter in court or walking through a divorce. Perhaps you lost your job or failed a class in school. Maybe you're overwhelmed by grief after losing a loved one. Or perhaps life has been hard and painful for so long that you don't see hope. As a believer, you can be confident that God will *orchestrate everything to work toward something good and beautiful.* Your job is to love Him and trust Him to do it.

DEAR LORD, YOU ARE GOOD ALL THE TIME. IN JESUS' NAME, AMEN.

It Starts with the Heart

Now you can have real love for everyone because your souls have been cleansed from selfishness and hatred when you trusted Christ to save you; so see to it that you really do love each other warmly, with all your hearts.

1 PETER 1:22 TLB

When you become a follower of Jesus, everything changes in you, starting with your heart. It's no longer all about your needs and wants. Instead, that selfishness becomes selflessness. The internal warfare becomes worship. Your anger subsides and is replaced by adoration. Hatred melts away as humility grows. Your capacity to love with passion and purpose begins to take over.

Friend, it's time to become a lover of people. Show kindness and generosity to those around you. Love even when it's difficult because God commands it. Even more, He will bless it. Cultivate genuine compassion and care for your community of friends and family, being an encouragement when they need it most.

DEAR LORD, CLEANSE MY HEART SO I CAN LOVE BETTER. IN JESUS' NAME, AMEN.

The Call to Stop Hating

"Do not take revenge on others or continue to hate them, but love your neighbors as you love yourself. I am the LORD."

LEVITICUS 19:18 GNT

If scripture says we're not to continue hating, that must mean hating happens. God created us with real human emotions that often get out of hand. We overuse them or underuse them. We respond in the wrong ways. But the hope is that these human emotions are quickly recognized and replaced with love. We can trust the Holy Spirit to nudge us when we're entertaining anger and bitterness.

How can you love those who make you angry? Start by praying, asking God to change your heart by letting go of any offenses. Pray for peace to reign over the situation. Pray for restoration and the spirit of reconciliation. Commit to keeping quiet rather than telling others you've been wronged. God knows. He will listen and empower you to forgive and love.

DEAR LORD, HELP ME PRAY FOR THOSE WHO HURT ME. IN JESUS' NAME, AMEN.

Loving Through God's Strength

"You have heard that it was said, 'Love your friends, hate your enemies.' But now I tell you: love your enemies and pray for those who persecute you."

MATTHEW 5:43–44 GNT

Today's verses reveal differences between living sacred lives and secular ones. As believers, we're called to live in ways that can seem upside down with the world's ideals. But when we accepted the gift of Jesus and decided to follow His commands, it included a desire for transformation. We wanted to be different.

Rather than only loving the lovable, we're called to love those who make it difficult. From the coworker who takes credit for your work, to the neighbor who lets their dog yap endlessly, to the friend who shares your secrets, to the parent who only offers critical words, sometimes it takes God's strength to choose love. The hurt may still be there, but He will bring comfort and healing. He will fortify you for forgiveness.

DEAR LORD, HELP ME LOVE THROUGH YOUR STRENGTH. IN JESUS' NAME, AMEN.

Shining God's Love

"You are the world's light—a city on a hill, glowing in the night for all to see. Don't hide your light! Let it shine for all; let your good deeds glow for all to see, so that they will praise your heavenly Father."

MATTHEW 5:14–16 TLB

How you live matters. Your life is your testimony, whether it's a good message or not. The words you use and the ways you act are revealing. They don't go unnoticed by others. Since we are to be the world's light, letting our lives point to God in heaven, let's make sure we lead with love.

Show generosity to the needy. Be kind to strangers. Find ways to compliment and encourage those around you. Put your needs last and be quick to offer help. Be humble and not boastful. Commit yourself to prayer and step into situations when you can provide what's needed. Friend, shine God's love into the world wherever possible.

DEAR LORD, I WANT TO SHINE YOUR LIGHT INTO A DARK WORLD. IN JESUS' NAME, AMEN.

Who Are the Unlovables?

"If you love only those who love you, what good is that? Even scoundrels do that much. If you are friendly only to your friends, how are you different from anyone else? Even the heathen do that."

MATTHEW 5:46–47 TLB

This is a challenge to love bigger. It's a call to love more broadly. It's a command not to be complacent and take the easy way out. God wants us to dig deeper and trust Him for the strength to love those who make it feel impossible.

Who are the unlovable people in your life? Who annoys you at every turn? Who regularly hurts your feelings and makes you feel worthless? Who rarely shows care or concern about your life? And who is hypercritical, leaving you feeling like a failure? Friend, these are those whom God calls us to love. Ask Him to tender your heart so you can extend grace and treat them with respect, even through healthy boundaries.

DEAR LORD, EMPOWER ME TO LOVE THOSE WHO MAKE IT DIFFICULT. IN JESUS' NAME, AMEN.

Let God Teach You to Love

But concerning the pure brotherly love that there should be among God's people, I don't need to say very much, I'm sure! For God himself is teaching you to love one another.
1 THESSALONIANS 4:9 TLB

Loving others comes easily. . .until it doesn't. Love feels effortless when everyone is playing nice and treating each other with kindness. It can be uncomplicated to show compassion to those who show it back. When they don't, we get tripped up.

Look to God when it feels challenging. Scripture says He will teach us. We can dig into the Bible to discover His thoughts on love. We can read the ways He demonstrates love. We can even learn how to increase our ability to show compassion and express kindness when it's the last thing we want to do. And we can pray for the Holy Spirit to grow the fruit of love in us so we can obey God's command.

DEAR LORD, TEACH ME HOW TO LOVE. IN JESUS' NAME, AMEN.

More and More

Indeed, your love is already strong toward all the Christian brothers throughout your whole nation. Even so, dear friends, we beg you to love them more and more.

1 THESSALONIANS 4:10 TLB

We're not only called to love others. . .but to love even more. We're to dig deeper, asking God to strengthen us to show compassion and care more meaningfully. We are to be more selfless. We are to show more kindness and generosity toward others. We're to extend grace quicker and work for reconciliation with one another. We must be more intentional in how we care for those around us. Our ability and willingness might already be strong, but the Lord wants it to be stronger.

Without His help, this won't happen. Our human limitations will ensure that truth. So, let's pray fervently, asking God for a more tender heart to love deeper. He will empower us to up our game so we can offer a more robust devotion.

DEAR LORD, SHOW ME HOW TO LOVE MORE. IN JESUS' NAME, AMEN.

A life of faith requires intentionality. It requires action and forward motion.

What Is Required

No, the L*ORD has told us what is good. What he requires of us is this: to do what is just, to show constant love, and to live in humble fellowship with our God.*

MICAH 6:8 GNT

While the sixth chapter in Micah is a conversation between God and the nation of Israel, believers today should follow the wisdom found in this verse. We can do *what is just* by knowing right from wrong, choosing what will bless others, and glorifying God. We can *show constant love* by offering loyal love and kindness to those around us as well as to the Lord. And we can *live in humble fellowship with God* by depending on Him for our needs rather than trying to work in our own strength.

A life of faith requires intentionality. It requires action and forward motion. Once we accept Jesus as our Savior, we are commanded to walk out a righteous life where loving others and God is expected.

DEAR LORD, HELP ME DO WHAT YOU REQUIRE. IN JESUS' NAME, AMEN.

Action-Inducing Faith

Suppose there are brothers or sisters who need clothes and don't have enough to eat. What good is there in your saying to them, "God bless you! Keep warm and eat well!"—if you don't give them the necessities of life? So it is with faith: if it is alone and includes no actions, then it is dead.

JAMES 2:15–17 GNT

Don't misunderstand what James is saying. We don't earn salvation through our works. Our actions should be a natural response to our faith. As believers, our hearts should be broken for what breaks God's. We should feel compassion toward the lost and those struggling. We should desire to help others, show gentleness when they're down, and be thoughtful when they are hurting. Our actions reveal what's in our hearts.

Let your faithful activities expose your deep love for the Lord. Live in ways that bless others, reminding them they're seen and known.

DEAR LORD, HELP ME LIVE MY FAITH OUT LOUD. IN JESUS' NAME, AMEN.

Loving Without Favoritism

Dear brothers, how can you claim that you belong to the Lord Jesus Christ, the Lord of glory, if you show favoritism to rich people and look down on poor people?

JAMES 2:1 TLB

Just as God never shows favoritism, neither should we. Our love should be the same for everyone. It shouldn't be dependent on anyone's financial status, race, education level, nationality, geographic location, skill set, skin color, likability, or anything else. These things only divide us from those we're called to love. Instead, we must remember who our Father is. God created everyone on purpose and for a purpose. Because we're in the family together, our love should flow equally to people of all kinds—just like His does.

What is the Holy Spirit speaking to you right now? Are there some areas where you need to recalibrate? Do you need to repent? Let God work in your heart, friend. He is ready and willing.

DEAR LORD, I CONFESS I'VE SHOWN FAVORITISM. HELP ME LOVE EVERYONE LIKE YOU DO. IN JESUS' NAME, AMEN.

Showing Selfless Love

Yes indeed, it is good when you truly obey our Lord's command, "You must love and help your neighbors just as much as you love and take care of yourself."

James 2:8 TLB

What a timely reminder that love isn't selfish. It's not self-focused. It doesn't demand its own needs be met first. Instead, when we obey God's command to love our neighbor like ourselves, love compels us to see their needs as equal to ours. We can be so quick to tend to our own needs first and foremost without looking up to see if anyone else needs support.

Ask God to open your eyes. Who is struggling? Who has too much on their plate? Who is grieving and could use practical help around the house? Who might be blessed with a home-cooked meal? Does someone need advice on moving forward? Does someone's medical condition require regular assistance? Where can you show selfless love in meaningful ways?

DEAR LORD, OPEN MY EYES SO I CAN LOVE WITH PURPOSE. IN JESUS' NAME, AMEN.

Reminders of His Love

Remind me each morning of your constant love, for I put my trust in you. My prayers go up to you; show me the way I should go.

PSALM 143:8 GNT

Maybe you're facing some difficult circumstances right now. You might be grieving the loss of someone important. Perhaps you lost your job or are very unhappy with the one you have. Maybe the natural consequences of your bad choices are catching up to you, and it's painful. Are you lonely? Do you feel rejected or abandoned? Has someone betrayed you? The best way to overcome these struggles is to remember that God deeply loves you.

Before your feet hit the floor each morning, ask the Lord to give you timely reminders of His love throughout the day. Remind yourself, especially when you're struggling the most. No matter what you are facing, God is bigger. Regardless of the pain, He is the healer.

DEAR LORD, THANK YOU FOR YOUR CONSTANT AND UNWAVERING LOVE. IN JESUS' NAME, AMEN.

Calling Sin Out in Love

My spiritual brothers and sisters, if one of our faithful has fallen into a trap and is snared by sin, don't stand idle and watch his demise. Gently restore him, being careful not to step into your own snare.

Galatians 6:1 voice

One of the most powerful ways to show others how much we care is by calling out their sin. When we do, it lets them know we love them too much to sit by and watch as they make foolish mistakes. Our approach should never be one of harsh criticism or judgment. Instead, it should be one of honest and loving concern. We want the best for those we care about.

In that same vein, be quick to recognize this compassionate act from those who love you. Frustration may come at first, but don't let it linger. Instead, see through the lens of love and be thankful you have friends and family willing to be honest.

DEAR LORD, HELP ME ACCEPT AND FACILITATE GENTLE RESTORATION. IN JESUS' NAME, AMEN.

Sharing in Each Other's Troubles

Share each other's troubles and problems, and so obey our Lord's command. If anyone thinks he is too great to stoop to this, he is fooling himself. He is really a nobody.

GALATIANS 6:2–3 TLB

Not only are we called to step into the mess with others, but we're to do so with the right attitude. The truth is that we're no better than anyone else. Our sin may just look different than theirs does. There will be times when our help is needed and other times when we're desperate for someone to help us navigate our own problems.

Approach these times with humility. Embrace the community you're part of, offering to help one another untangle the knots that life brings. Be full of compassion and genuine love. Let's be willing to get our hands dirty without spewing condemnation or criticism. We can invest in each other's lives as we walk out things together.

DEAR LORD, THANK YOU FOR COMMUNITY AND THE POWER IT BRINGS FOR BELIEVERS. IN JESUS' NAME, AMEN.

When You Have the Chance

So let us not become tired of doing good; for if we do not give up, the time will come when we will reap the harvest. So then, as often as we have the chance, we should do good to everyone, and especially to those who belong to our family in the faith.

Galatians 6:9–10 GNT

As often as you have the chance, you should demonstrate kindness and generosity to others, especially other believers. You should choose to love them through your time and treasure. You should be quick to forgive and work toward restoration. You should overlook offenses, so no walls are built between you and others. Be willing to get in the trenches and help others navigate tough seasons of life. Never tire to the point of walking away in exhaustion or frustration, because your perseverance will be rewarded.

Never tire of doing the right thing. Ask God for strength, vision, and endurance.

DEAR LORD, I KNOW YOU WILL SUSTAIN AND REFRESH ME TO LOVE OTHERS WELL. IN JESUS' NAME, AMEN.

Outdoing Others

In response to all he has done for us, let us outdo each other in being helpful and kind to each other and in doing good.
HEBREWS 10:24 TLB

If we're going to try to outdo anyone, let's try to trump them in how we show love to those around us. Let's be extra compassionate in helping the ones who need support. Let's work harder to make them feel special and important. We can show extravagant love through the words we speak and the things we do, careful to leave people better than when we found them. This persistent attitude infused by the Holy Spirit and fueled by faith in Jesus Christ helps us thrive at being helpful and kind rather than selfish.

Who needs your loving-kindness today? Where can you generously and humbly outdo the kind of care others are showing? What a privilege to be the hands and feet of Jesus to a broken and hurting world.

DEAR LORD, HELP ME LOVE LAVISHLY.
IN JESUS' NAME, AMEN.

The Power of Community

Let us not neglect our church meetings, as some people do, but encourage and warn each other, especially now that the day of his coming back again is drawing near.

HEBREWS 10:25 TLB

Community is a gift from the Lord because it helps us feel connected and valued. It enables us to find like-minded people working toward a common good. It can also help us grow and find encouragement along the way. Church communities, small groups, Bible studies, and service teams offer powerful opportunities to both experience kindness and share it. For some, church becomes family.

When we opt out of showing up in our community, we lose out on its goodness. They lose out on the love and talents we bring to the table, which is why scripture reminds us to stay connected. We need one another. As believers, we need the unique care and concern of other believers. It's biblical and a vital part of a solid life of faith.

DEAR LORD, HELP ME SEE COMMUNITY AS GOOD AND NECESSARY. IN JESUS' NAME, AMEN.

Love by Modeling

Don't let anyone belittle you because you are young. Instead, show the faithful, young and old, an example of how to live: set the standard for how to talk, act, love, and be faithful and pure.

1 TIMOTHY 4:12 VOICE

Timothy battled insecurity because of his age. He had an amazing call to love others by sharing the gospel, and Paul wanted to encourage his young friend to be bold in doing so, even if it was challenging. We can also let Paul's words encourage us today, making sure our age—young or old—doesn't stifle our desire to love others by showing them an example of faithful living.

This means we must recognize that our lives speak loudly. People are watching how we navigate the ups and downs that come our way. We have the honor and burden of loving them by modeling a righteous life they can imitate.

DEAR LORD, HELP ME SET THE STANDARD FOR HOW TO TALK, ACT, LOVE, AND BE FAITHFUL AND PURE. IN JESUS' NAME, AMEN.

Love should rule strong and bold in our hearts regardless of who is on the receiving end.

Leading with Love

Let love continue among you. Don't forget to extend your hospitality to all—even to strangers—for as you know, some have unknowingly shown kindness to heavenly messengers in this way.

HEBREWS 13:1–2 VOICE

How humbling to imagine we might encounter angels. Why do you think God would place them in our path? We don't know for sure, but maybe He does because they allow us to demonstrate the depth of our love. Perhaps they reveal what's in our hearts. Maybe they also expose if favoritism plays a role in our ability to show kindness to those we know and strangers alike.

Love should rule strong and bold in our hearts regardless of who is on the receiving end. Be it your father, sister, coworker, bestie, neighbor, a stranger in the store, or maybe even a heavenly messenger, lead with compassion. Treat others in the ways you'd like to be treated in return.

DEAR LORD, LET ME LEAD WITH LOVE IN EVERY INTERACTION. IN JESUS' NAME, AMEN.

Love Through Obedience

Obey your spiritual leaders and be willing to do what they say. For their work is to watch over your souls, and God will judge them on how well they do this. Give them reason to report joyfully about you to the Lord and not with sorrow, for then you will suffer for it too.

HEBREWS 13:17 TLB

God is a big proponent of obedience. Throughout the Bible, He points to it as a demonstration of love. Following His commands reveals allegiance and adoration, and it doesn't go unnoticed. When you follow His chosen ones—like they did in biblical times with Moses, David, and the prophets—He sees that too. If you desire to show God how much you love Him, obey authority.

As believers today, when we listen to our spiritual leaders, it affirms them and speaks volumes to the Father. Their work is to watch over us, and our obedience proves their effectiveness in doing what God has asked.

DEAR LORD, I WILL OBEY BECAUSE I LOVE YOU. IN JESUS' NAME, AMEN.

Loving with Precision

Let us give thanks to the God and Father of our Lord Jesus Christ, the merciful Father, the God from whom all help comes! He helps us in all our troubles, so that we are able to help others who have all kinds of troubles, using the same help that we ourselves have received from God.

2 Corinthians 1:3–4 GNT

In His loving-kindness, God comforts us in our trials. He helps us walk through dark valleys and wade through tumultuous waters. The Lord strengthens us. He imparts wisdom and discernment. God reminds us of our value to Him and others. He settles our anxious hearts and brings hope. We learn from His care to offer our friends and family the same comfort.

We can love with precision because we have learned from the best. We can help others in their troubling circumstances, showing compassion in ways that matter most because God has done that for us.

DEAR LORD, THANK YOU FOR TEACHING ME TO LOVE. IN JESUS' NAME, AMEN.

His Compassion Never Ends

Yet there is one ray of hope: his compassion never ends. It is only the Lord's mercies that have kept us from complete destruction. Great is his faithfulness; his loving-kindness begins afresh each day.

LAMENTATIONS 3:21–23 TLB

What a relief to know that God's compassion is forever. There's nothing we can do to remove it from our lives, even when we're disobedient and not following His will and plan. His kindness is constant, and His care is endless. Friend, God's love for you is relentless.

Ask the Lord to make this beautiful truth real to you every day. Ask Him to make it come alive within you. We need Him to take that reality from our heads and sink it into our hearts. Because if we truly believed it, our responses to life would look much different. We'd be bold and brave in our decisions. If we knew the depth of God's love, it would change everything.

DEAR LORD, HELP ME BETTER UNDERSTAND THE UNENDING LOVE YOU HAVE FOR ME. IN JESUS' NAME, AMEN.

Earthly Father Versus Heavenly Father

But Lord, You are a God full of compassion, generous in grace, slow to anger, and boundless in loyal love and truth.

Psalm 86:15 voice

Friend, your heavenly Father is everything you'd ever want or need. While you may be frustrated and unsatisfied with your earthly father, know the Lord will always make up the difference.

He offers compassion with a fullness that cannot be matched. His grace is generously given without question. God's anger comes slowly because His patience is enduring. His love is faithful and reliable, proving His unwavering devotion. The Lord's Word is steadfast truth that can be trusted. Don't let your childhood dad skew your perception of your eternal one. Instead, recognize his faults and limitations and let God heal your heart as He reminds you that He is the perfect Father who will never disappoint or discourage you.

DEAR LORD, THANK YOU FOR BEING EVERYTHING MY EARTHLY DAD COULD NOT BE. HELP ME EXTEND GRACE AND EMBRACE YOUR GOODNESS. IN JESUS' NAME, AMEN.

Living Others-Focused

"Long ago I gave these commands to my people: 'You must see that justice is done, and must show kindness and mercy to one another. Do not oppress widows, orphans, foreigners who live among you, or anyone else in need. And do not plan ways of harming one another.'"

ZECHARIAH 7:9–10 GNT

God wants us to be good and caring humans. He wants our hearts to overflow with the desire to treat others respectfully and kindly. His plan is for believers to have a solid moral compass so the underserved and disenfranchised find hope. We're to have a sense of justice, righting wrongs in the world according to the Lord's will. We are called to love lavishly in all we do—even when tough love is needed.

Sometimes this feels organic. It feels effortless. But at other times, living this way requires us to stop being self-focused and choose to be focused on others. Ask God for the strength.

DEAR LORD, LET ME SEE THE NEEDS OF OTHERS AND OFFER TO HELP. IN JESUS' NAME, AMEN.

You Are Unforgettable

Is it possible for a mother, however disappointed, however hurt, to forget her nursing child? Can she feel nothing for the baby she carried and birthed? Even if she could, I, God, will never forget you.

Isaiah 49:15 VOICE

This verse tries to help us understand the depth of God's love by reminding us of the powerful connection between a mother and her child. Whether you have first-hand knowledge of this parenting bond or not, you can recognize its formidableness. Friend, the Lord's love for you is even stronger.

You may feel unloved or unwanted by the world. You may feel unseen or unheard by those around you. You may even feel rejected and abandoned by those you trusted. But the love God has for you is unshakable. To Him, you are unforgettable. Rest in that truth, and let it bolster your confidence today. Nothing can separate you from the Father's care.

DEAR LORD, WHAT A BLESSING TO KNOW THAT YOU FULLY AND COMPLETELY LOVE ME. IN JESUS' NAME, AMEN.

Pure Love

Now the Lord is not slow about enacting His promise—
slow is how some people want to characterize it—no,
He is not slow but patient and merciful to you, not wanting
anyone to be destroyed, but wanting everyone to turn away
from following his own path and to turn toward God's.

2 PETER 3:9 VOICE

Have you ever said in frustration, "Come Lord Jesus!" Maybe you've looked at the state of the world and wondered why He is still seated in the heavens. Chances are you have prayed earnestly for His return to come sooner rather than later. Yet here we are.

Consider that it's because of the Lord's great love that He is patient. It's His mercy at work. God waits because He wants everyone to accept the gift of salvation and spend eternity in heaven. His timing is purposeful and perfect. This isn't forgetfulness or slothfulness; this is pure love for His creation.

DEAR LORD, I TRUST YOUR TIMING IN ALL THINGS. IN JESUS' NAME, AMEN.

Showing Our Love

Dear friends, while you are waiting for these things to happen and for him to come, try hard to live without sinning; and be at peace with everyone so that he will be pleased with you when he returns.

2 Peter 3:14 TLB

Until we see Jesus face-to-face, the best way we can show our love is to live a righteous life that pleases Him. Our obedience reveals our devotion. Each time we choose God's way over our own—setting aside our fleshly, self-serving desires—it lets Him know we're serious about living correctly. We can also delight His heart by doing our best to get along with others and extend kindness and compassion. Yes, how we navigate our short time here matters to God.

So, let's be women who want to please the Lord with our words and actions. If He asks it, let's do it. Let's clothe ourselves in love for the Father and others.

DEAR LORD, UNTIL I SEE YOUR FACE, LET ME SHOW LOVE TO YOU AND OTHERS. IN JESUS' NAME, AMEN.

He Gets It

For Jesus is not some high priest who has no sympathy for our weaknesses and flaws. He has already been tested in every way that we are tested; but He emerged victorious, without failing God.

HEBREWS 4:15 VOICE

Jesus has sympathy for us because He gets it. He has a first-hand understanding of our human limitations. As Christ walked the earth, He faced the kind of trials we face today. He was tempted and taunted, just like us. In His flesh, Jesus overcame them all. What a blessing to know our Lord cared enough to walk in our shoes and make way for an eternity in heaven. We are known and loved.

That means we have an ally to help us walk through this life. When we pray, He has compassion because Jesus knows the weaknesses and flaws of humanity. Be honest about your struggles. With His earthly experiences and divine Lordship, let Him help you navigate each step.

DEAR LORD, I LOVE THAT YOU UNDERSTAND THE CHALLENGES I FACE EVERY DAY. IN JESUS' NAME, AMEN.

Invited to the Throne Room

So let us step boldly to the throne of grace, where we can find mercy and grace to help when we need it most.
Hebrews 4:16 voice

As believers, and because of God's deep compassion and love, we can pray directly to Him about whatever is on our hearts. What you need is important. He wants to hear about the challenges you're facing. The Lord is always listening and available to help those who ask. So, friend, what do you need?

Do you need grace for an annoying coworker or perspective regarding a confusing situation? Are you at a crossroads and need wisdom and discernment for the next right step? Do you crave God's comfort as you grieve or His strength as you battle fear? Or do you need to confess and repent so nothing stands in the way of your relationship with the Lord? You are invited to the throne room, beloved.

DEAR LORD, THANK YOU FOR INVITING ME TO PRAY DIRECTLY TO YOU WITH MY NEEDS. IN JESUS' NAME, AMEN.

Loving, Not Judging

"Do not judge others, so that God will not judge you, for God will judge you in the same way you judge others, and he will apply to you the same rules you apply to others."

MATTHEW 7:1–2 GNT

If we follow God's command to love our neighbors as we love ourselves, we'll be less tempted to judge others. Instead, we'll be more interested in extending kindness and grace. We will want to make sure they feel loved and seen through our words and actions. We will want to live at peace with them and serve them as needed. Focusing on the Lord's command to love profoundly benefits us too.

Have you been critical of someone lately? Do you tend to belittle others when they don't do things your way? Do you pass judgment quickly? Take heed of today's verses and let them keep you from speaking or thinking negatively about those around you, lest you face the same treatment.

DEAR LORD, HELP ME LOVE AND NOT JUDGE. IN JESUS' NAME, AMEN.

If we follow God's command to love our neighbors as we love ourselves, we'll be less tempted to judge others.

When You Focus on Shortcomings

"How can you say to another believer, 'Let me take the piece of sawdust out of your eye,' when you have a beam in your own eye? You hypocrite! First remove the beam from your own eye. Then you will see clearly to remove the piece of sawdust from another believer's eye."

MATTHEW 7:4–5 GW

It's easy to focus on what others are doing wrong without also recognizing where we're falling short. We can be quick to point out their failure and not see our own. We adopt a critical posture while thinking we are flawless (or close to it). This is unloving.

Humility is the gateway to compassion. When we understand our own wretchedness without Jesus, it keeps us modest. An unpretentious attitude makes us approachable and helps create trust in relationships. Choosing to overlook their *sawdust* because we're fully aware of our *beam* and simply showing love is a beautiful gift.

DEAR LORD, HELP ME NOT FOCUS ON WHERE OTHERS FALL SHORT, BUT LOVE THEM INSTEAD. IN JESUS' NAME, AMEN.

Do to Others

This is what our Scriptures come to teach:
in everything, in every circumstance,
do to others as you would have them do to you.
MATTHEW 7:12 VOICE

If you want to be loved, then show others they are loved. If you want to feel compassion when life gets hard, then demonstrate that to those around you. If you're looking for loyal friends, then be one. If you want honest relationships full of integrity, then lead the way. Scripture is clear that we're to treat others how we want them to treat us.

This doesn't guarantee results, however. It's not a magical formula that works flawlessly. But when we intentionally show concern for others with all forms of kindness and generosity, it speaks loudly and sets us up to receive that same treatment in return. Knowing that, handle others with care. Be tender with their feelings. Appreciate who God made them to be.

DEAR LORD, HELP ME BE A WOMAN WHO LOVES OTHERS IN WAYS I WANT TO BE LOVED. IN JESUS' NAME, AMEN.

You're Fully Loved

Even if the mountains heave up from their anchors, and the hills quiver and shake, I will not desert you. You can rely on My enduring love; My covenant of peace will stand forever. So says the Eternal One, whose love won't give up on you.

ISAIAH 54:10 VOICE

Let this verse settle your anxious heart today. Let it quiet the voices that tell you God's love is something that must be earned and that can be taken away. Be assured that His promises made are promises kept, without fail, and for generations to come. Know that no matter what you do or how badly you mess up, nothing could make the Lord love you any more or any less than He does at this very moment. His love is stable and unending.

What is your response to this powerful truth? How does it bring peace and comfort? Where are you struggling to believe it?

DEAR LORD, HELP ME BELIEVE TODAY'S VERSE WITH EVERY FIBER OF MY BEING. IN JESUS' NAME, AMEN.

Operating Differently

He is merciful and tender toward those who don't deserve it; he is slow to get angry and full of kindness and love. He never bears a grudge, nor remains angry forever.

PSALM 103:8–9 TLB

In a world of hot heads and quick tempers, isn't it reassuring to know that God operates differently? We're used to people being easily frustrated when things don't go their way. They seem irritated and annoyed over trivial things, and anger grows from there. Whether by design or by accident, all tenderness and kindness dissipate, leaving us hurt.

Let's follow God's example from today's verses and choose to operate differently too. With His help, we can extend grace to slow our anger. We can pray for patience daily. Instead of taking our struggles out on the people around us, we can take them to the Lord. Let's learn to show mercy and tenderness, choosing to love with great purpose.

DEAR LORD, SHOW ME HOW TO SLOW MY ANGER AND OPERATE DIFFERENTLY LIKE YOU DO. IN JESUS' NAME, AMEN.

Returning to the Father

So he got up and returned to his father. The father looked off in the distance and saw the young man returning. He felt compassion for his son and ran out to him, enfolded him in an embrace, and kissed him.

Luke 15:20 VOICE

This son was no saint. He had asked for his inheritance early and squandered every bit without discernment. He was selfish and followed the wiles of his heart. When he went home—broke and beaten down—no doubt he expected a dismal response from his father. But that's not what he received.

God is represented by the dad in this verse, and his reaction to the prodigal son's return is how the Father feels when we come back to Him. Do you need to repent, friend? Do you want to return to God? He is waiting for you, watching for you, and ready to embrace you with great compassion and love.

DEAR LORD, THANK YOU FOR ALWAYS WELCOMING ME HOME WITH OPEN ARMS FULL OF LOVE. IN JESUS' NAME, AMEN.

Let It Seep In

As he came near the entrance to the city, he met a funeral procession. The dead man was a widow's only child. A large crowd from the city was with her. When the Lord saw her, he felt sorry for her. He said to her, "Don't cry."

Luke 7:12–13 GW

It's wonderful to read about those moments of compassion in the Bible. What a blessing to understand the goodness of the Lord and see His tender heart at work. Friend, God included those snapshots for a reason. We're meant to read and learn more about Him. He reveals Himself in scripture, which is designed to deepen our love toward Him and solidify our devotion to a life of faith. Because we know God is unchangeable, the compassion He felt for this mother is the same compassion He has for us.

Embrace His love today. Let it seep into every nook and cranny of your heart and satisfy.

DEAR LORD, ENABLE YOUR LOVE TO PENETRATE MY HEART PROFOUNDLY. IN JESUS' NAME, AMEN.

Sharing Your Faith

Therefore, now no condemnation awaits those who are living in Jesus the Anointed, the Liberating King, because when you live in the Anointed One, Jesus, a new law takes effect. The law of the Spirit of life breathes into you and liberates you from the law of sin and death.

ROMANS 8:1–2 VOICE

As a believer whose eternity in heaven is secured through the blood of Jesus, you will experience no condemnation from the Lord. Holy Spirit conviction, yes. But condemnation, no. Your decision to follow Christ removed His judgment once and for all. Accepting Jesus as your personal Savior ushers in a new freedom from guilt and shame. God's love liberated you.

When you love others, you'll also want this same blessing for them. Ask the Lord to embolden you to share your faith when the doors of opportunity open. Let your compassion for the lost and broken lead them to Jesus.

DEAR LORD, IT MAKES ME NERVOUS TO SHARE MY FAITH. GIVE ME LOVE AND COURAGE TO DO IT ANYWAY. IN JESUS' NAME, AMEN.

Payback

When you give to the poor, it is like lending to the Lord, and the Lord will pay you back.

Proverbs 19:17 GNT

God sees it when you are kind to those who are lacking. When you are generous with your finances or love people with your time, it doesn't go unnoticed. The Lord is delighted. He promises to reward your compassion in His perfect timing.

Are there people in your life who need some loving-kindness? Who is struggling to make ends meet? Is anyone in your community of friends and family oppressed or beaten down by life? Who could use unexpected goodness? Listen for the Spirit's voice, directing you to support them in specific ways, and ask God to show you the next right step. When you commit to blessing others, you love them according to His plan. He will pay you back.

DEAR LORD, I WANT MY LIFE TO GLORIFY YOU AND BLESS OTHERS. HELP ME SEE WHEN THERE'S A NEED AND GIVE ME THE DESIRE TO MEET IT. IN JESUS' NAME, AMEN.

Asking Questions

When Jesus came to the place where they were, he stopped in the road and called, "What do you want me to do for you?" "Sir," they said, "we want to see!" Jesus was moved with pity for them and touched their eyes. And instantly they could see, and followed him.

MATTHEW 20:32–34 TLB

There are times we feel paralyzed to help others. We want to; we're just not sure what to do. We may not know their most significant or most pressing needs. Instead of stepping up to offer support or asking how we can help, we shrink in confusion.

Jesus asked, "What do you want me to do for you?" Of course, He knew their needs, but He allowed them to respond. His question revealed His compassion. What if we loved in the same way? Let's be willing to get in the trenches with others and do whatever needs to be done.

DEAR LORD, ENCOURAGE ME TO SUPPORT OTHERS ACCORDING TO THEIR NEEDS AND YOUR WILL. IN JESUS' NAME, AMEN.

Simply Put, Choose Love

"Happy are those who are merciful to others; God will be merciful to them! Happy are the pure in heart; they will see God! Happy are those who work for peace; God will call them his children!"

MATTHEW 5:7–9 GNT

Do you see the connection? When we love others and treat them with kindness and compassion, we receive a blessing for doing so. God sees our hearts and genuine motives and gives us His goodness in return. A divine gift awaits those who choose to be the Lord's hands and feet.

So, friend, be generous to those around you in the ways God commands. Extend grace rather than keep a scorecard of offenses. Show mercy and benevolence when possible. Love with authenticity and without selfish interests. Find a path to live peaceably and work at it with diligence. Simply put, choose love. And then watch as the Lord blesses your obedience.

DEAR LORD, HELP ME CHOOSE LOVE WHENEVER POSSIBLE, FOLLOWING YOUR COMMAND BY FAITH. IN JESUS' NAME, AMEN.

His Comfort and Compassion

Sing for joy, O heavens; shout, O earth. Break forth with song, O mountains, for the Lord has comforted his people and will have compassion upon them in their sorrow.

Isaiah 49:13 TLB

Where do you need God's compassion today? Where do you need Him to show unwavering faithfulness? Throughout the Bible, scripture is clear that God brings both comfort and love when we need it most. He is the source who will meet our every need. When we find ourselves overwhelmed and discouraged, we can go directly to Him.

Is work extra challenging right now? Has a close friend let you down? Are you fighting with family members because of unmet expectations? Did the doctor's report come back with worrisome issues? Are you feeling lonely and unseen? Are you dealing with the consequences of a moral failure? Go to God in prayer and let His love wrap around you, settling your spirit and calming your anxious heart.

DEAR LORD, YOU ARE ALL I NEED.
IN JESUS' NAME, AMEN.

Big or Small

One day about this time as another great crowd gathered, the people ran out of food again. Jesus called his disciples to discuss the situation. "I pity these people," he said, "for they have been here three days and have nothing left to eat."

MARK 8:1–2 TLB

Today's verses show that the Lord cares about the big things you're navigating and the small, practical ones too. His compassion covers everything from the pile of bills to the argument with a coworker, a bout with insecurity, and a hunger pang. If it matters to you, it matters to Him.

It can be hard to feel worthy of such encompassing love. Based on your life experiences, it can also be hard to imagine someone caring that much. But the truth is the truth, and there's nothing that can change it. Let God be the one who you run to for everything—big or small—because He cares about every bit of it.

DEAR LORD, I'M HUMBLED BY THE DEPTH OF YOUR LOVE. IN JESUS' NAME, AMEN.

Let Love Be a Verb

Even his own neighbors despise the poor man, while the rich have many "friends." But to despise the poor is to sin. Blessed are those who help them.

PROVERBS 14:20–21 TLB

We should always be looking for ways to help others. Whether a stranger or someone we know, if there is a way for us to show support, it's God's desire that we engage. The problem is, however, that we don't always want to. Sometimes the last thing on our long to-do list is coming to the aid of another. So, what do we do?

Start each morning with prayer. Ask the Lord to open your heart to serve others in need. Spend time in the Word, learning more about what God expects from believers. Practice kindness. Look for ways you can bless others, be it simple or more involved. Let love be a verb, an action step you take each day to love someone with purpose.

DEAR LORD, TEACH ME HOW TO SHOWCASE LOVE IN ACTION. IN JESUS' NAME, AMEN.

Let love be a verb,
an action step you
take each day to love
someone with purpose.

Leaning into God

Wherever they are, they will be fine, never hungry nor thirsty. They will be protected from oppressive heat and the burning sun because the One who loves them—as a mother loves her child—will be their guide. God will lead them to restful places, rejuvenating springs of water.

Isaiah 49:10 voice

God will always take care of those He loves. There is no distance that can keep Him away. There's no problem we face that He cannot solve. Nothing can stand in the way of the Lord's care and concern. He is our protector, our strong tower, our source, our Creator, and the one who will never turn from us.

In a world that offers only conditional love, lean into God when you're feeling overwhelmed and discouraged. Let Him guide you into restful places where He'll restore you from weariness. Let the Lord speak into those parched places and bring them back to life.

DEAR LORD, YOU ALWAYS KNOW WHAT'S BEST FOR ME. LET ME REST IN YOUR LOVE ALONE. IN JESUS' NAME, AMEN.

Loving God's Way

Stay always within the boundaries where God's love can reach and bless you. Wait patiently for the eternal life that our Lord Jesus Christ in his mercy is going to give you. Try to help those who argue against you. Be merciful to those who doubt.

JUDE 21–22 TLB

Today's verse tells us to stay within the boundaries of our faith, offer to help those who are difficult, and show compassion to doubters. Do you recognize that these commands require great intentionality? These are not routine tasks, especially as we sometimes go through the day on autopilot. We must be deliberate to make good choices that will honor others and bring glory to God. How do we do this?

If we desire to show love as He commands, and we pray each day for guidance, the Holy Spirit will prompt us to obey. As we spend time in the Word, committed to living out what we read, His voice will bring reminders.

DEAR LORD, STRENGTHEN ME TO LOVE YOUR WAY. IN JESUS' NAME, AMEN.

Loving Their Differences

That way there should be no division in the body; instead, all the parts mutually depend on and care for one another. If one part is suffering, then all the members suffer alongside it. If one member is honored, then all the members celebrate alongside it.

1 CORINTHIANS 12:25–26 VOICE

We love others by being an agent of harmony. We show genuine respect for what makes others different by understanding we each bring something unique into the mix. Rather than focusing on those variances as unfavorable, God wants us to see how we all fit together into His plan.

Community is essential to the Father because we're created for it. We're to depend on one another and compassionately support each other through the ups and downs. Who are the people God has put into your life, and how can you better demonstrate your love for them?

DEAR LORD, EQUIP ME TO SHOW GENUINE LOVE AND BRING A SPIRIT OF UNITY TO MY COMMUNITY. IN JESUS' NAME, AMEN.

Sharing Your Gift

Each believer has received a gift that manifests the Spirit's power and presence. That gift is given for the good of the whole community.

1 CORINTHIANS 12:7 VOICE

When you accepted Jesus as your Savior, God gave you a beautiful gift to share with others. He did the same for every other believer. The Holy Spirit in you brings it to life and gives it power. This gift is how you express love for God and compassion for others. It's meant to be shared with your community of friends and family.

Sometimes, we tend to stay quiet and keep our faith to ourselves. Maybe we're shy or feel intimidated by other more seasoned believers. But when we do this, we're robbing those around us of the goodness God instilled in us. He gave us something to reveal, not to hide. Ask the Holy Spirit for the confidence to display your gift as you love your community through it.

DEAR LORD, GIVE ME THE COURAGE TO SHARE THE GIFT YOU'VE GIVEN ME. IN JESUS' NAME, AMEN.

The Choice to Forgive

"If you forgive others the wrongs they have done to you, your Father in heaven will also forgive you. But if you do not forgive others, then your Father will not forgive the wrongs you have done."

MATTHEW 6:14–15 GNT

One of the most powerful ways you can show love is to simply forgive. While it may not be the easiest of decisions, it's a mighty one that packs a punch. When you choose to extend grace rather than hold a grudge, it delights the Lord because it reveals the condition of your heart.

Choosing forgiveness doesn't negate your feelings or mean you weren't legitimately wronged. It doesn't mean they're off the hook from natural consequences. It also doesn't mean that God won't deal with them at some point. Your forgiveness is obedience, plain and simple. Your humble obedience proves your love for the Lord and for the one who hurt you.

DEAR LORD, LET ME BE QUICK TO SHOW LOVE THROUGH FORGIVENESS. IN JESUS' NAME, AMEN.

Checking Your Motives

"But when you help a needy person, do it in such a way that even your closest friend will not know about it. Then it will be a private matter. And your Father, who sees what you do in private, will reward you."

MATTHEW 6:3–4 GNT

Don't get tangled in the idea that others must see your acts of love as a measurement of your goodness. It's a slippery slope when you desire recognition for being kind and generous. Check your motives when you want to give so others can see it, for it may be a red flag or warning. Instead, let your show of compassion be done in humility.

We are called to be a blessing in many ways. Sometimes, it's with our time or prayers. Other times, it's with our financial or material resources. Regardless of how we serve, it's worth remembering that God isn't impressed when we parade our acts of love to garner attention.

DEAR LORD, HELP ME LOVE IN HUMILITY AND WITH THE RIGHT MOTIVES. IN JESUS' NAME, AMEN.

Loving Without Judgment

When Pharaoh's daughter opened the basket, she found the baby boy. He was crying, and her heart melted with compassion.
Pharoah's Daughter: *This is a Hebrew child.*

Exodus 2:6 voice

What a gift that God included this verse in the Bible. It's such a beautiful reminder that we can (and should) love each other regardless of skin color, nationality, financial or social status, or anything else. There's nothing that should stunt our ability to show compassion to one another. We are all God's creation and deserve to experience love and kindness.

If you're struggling to walk this out, talk to the Lord about it. Be honest about where the challenges are for you. Ask Him to change your heart so you can love others with His divine strength and perspective. Friend, if God can tender the heart of an Egyptian princess to have compassion on a Hebrew child, He can do the same for you.

DEAR LORD, GIVE ME THE CAPACITY TO LOVE OTHERS NO MATTER WHAT. IN JESUS' NAME, AMEN.

Bringing Encouragement

So support one another. Keep building each other up as you have been doing.
1 THESSALONIANS 5:11 VOICE

Take a moment to consider those friends and family members who may need an extra dose of encouragement today. Who in your circle could use meaningful support right now, be it emotionally, physically, or financially? Where would your time and effort make a difference in the life of another? Loving often means putting their needs ahead of yours and being the hands and feet of Jesus. It means supporting even when it's inconvenient. That is exactly what God wants us to do.

Ask the Lord to put people on your heart, and then be thoughtful in how you can impact them. What is He asking you to do? What is the Holy Spirit's prompting? What is the timeline for your engagement? Where can you best meet their needs? How can you shine hope into their circumstances? Let's be women who have faith with feet, bringing encouragement when possible.

DEAR LORD, USE ME TO BRING HOPE! IN JESUS' NAME, AMEN.

Showing Love Through Appreciation

Brothers and sisters, we ask you to show appreciation to those who are working hard among you and those who are your leaders as they guide and instruct you in the Lord—they are priceless. When you think about them, let it be with great love in your heart because of all the work they have done. Let peace live and reign among you.

1 THESSALONIANS 5:12–13 VOICE

Every day, you have the opportunity to show others genuine love through heartfelt appreciation. There is such goodness in letting someone know that you're grateful for their help and guidance. It makes a difference! It's important to thank those who have taken the time to bless you. You can even show gratitude to someone just for being who God created them to be. Whenever you get the chance, express love with a glad heart.

DEAR LORD, THERE IS SO MUCH TO BE THANKFUL FOR AND WONDERFUL PEOPLE WHO DESERVE MY APPRECIATION. HELP ME HAVE A GLAD HEART AND LOVE THEM WELL. IN JESUS' NAME, AMEN.

Engaged in Community

Brothers and sisters, we strongly advise you to scold the rebels who devote their lives to wreaking havoc, to encourage the downcast, to help the sick and weak, and to be patient with all of them.

1 THESSALONIANS 5:14 VOICE

We have many roles to play in the community of friends and family surrounding us. From calling people out for bad behavior to bringing hope to the hopeless to caring for those with health challenges, we're to be deeply involved with those around us. We're to be directly connected and working together to create a wonderful community where we can love each other and thrive.

We may have a tendency to put others on the back burner because of a busy schedule or contribute only when it's convenient, but that's not what God is asking. Instead, He wants us to be actively engaged and devoted in meaningful ways that let others know they matter.

DEAR LORD, LET ME SHOW LOVE TO MY COMMUNITY SO THEY FEEL VALUED. IN JESUS' NAME, AMEN.

Life is hard enough.
Let's demonstrate
love to others
whenever possible.

Aiming to Do Good

See that no one pays back wrong for wrong, but at all times make it your aim to do good to one another and to all people.

1 THESSALONIANS 5:15 GNT

We may not be perfect, but we can choose to live life in purposeful ways. We can be aware of how we're treating others and aim to do better when we fall short. We can stop vengeful thoughts from forming into action plans and instead take that pain to the Lord.

God commands us to love everyone, which includes aiming to do good to one another. Again, perfection isn't the goal. We're human and flawed. But we can make wise, compassionate choices in how we interact with those around us. As we prayerfully ask the Lord for the strength to show kindness and be considerate, the Holy Spirit will enable us to do so. Life is hard enough. Let's demonstrate love to others whenever possible.

DEAR LORD, KEEP MY HEART TENDER SO I DESIRE TO TREAT OTHERS WELL. IN JESUS' NAME, AMEN.

A Grateful Heart

Always be joyful. Always keep on praying.
No matter what happens, always be thankful,
for this is God's will for you who belong to Christ Jesus.
1 THESSALONIANS 5:16–18 TLB

A grateful heart is a powerful part of living a life of faith. It helps us keep the proper perspective on who God is. It keeps us humble and pliable. Gratitude ushers in joy, even in the most challenging situations. It helps us look for the silver linings that are always present. It keeps our hearts full of love to share with others. Most importantly, it's God's will.

One way to maintain a thankful posture is to show appreciation to the Lord in prayer. Scripture tells us all good things come from above (James 1:17), so there's no shortage of reasons to say. . .*Thank You*. Tell God you love Him for taking such good care of you.

DEAR LORD, FORGIVE ME FOR NOT SHOWING GRATITUDE WHEN I SHOULD HAVE. HELP ME SEE YOUR GOODNESS AND BE QUICK TO THANK YOU FOR IT. IN JESUS' NAME, AMEN.

Sharing the Gospel

"Wherever you go, make disciples of all nations: Baptize them in the name of the Father, and of the Son, and of the Holy Spirit. Teach them to do everything I have commanded you. And remember that I am always with you until the end of time."

MATTHEW 28:19–20 GW

One of the most extraordinary acts of love we can extend to others is sharing the gospel with them. Teaching about Jesus and leading them into a saving faith changes their life here and in eternity. As we walk out our faith together with the Lord, offering encouragement and guidance along the way, He is glorified and we are blessed.

Ask God for the courage and confidence to testify how His goodness has manifested in your life. Let Him empower you to speak up when the opportunity arises. Love others enough to lead them to Jesus.

DEAR LORD, HELP ME OBEY YOUR COMMAND TO MAKE DISCIPLES, ENCOURAGING THEM TO FOLLOW YOUR WILL AND WAYS. IN JESUS' NAME, AMEN.

Focusing on Others

We should stop looking out for our own interests and instead focus on the people living and breathing around us.

1 CORINTHIANS 10:24 VOICE

Today's verse is a challenge to be selfless rather than selfish. It's a call to put others ahead of yourself and focus on their needs instead of always looking out for number one. It's about showing intentional compassion toward friends and family, looking for ways you can support them. It's following God's command to love in meaningful and significant ways.

Today, ask the Lord to open your eyes. Who needs help moving? Who could use a home-cooked meal? Who is struggling to make ends meet? How can you show care and concern to your neighbors or coworkers? Where can you bless your roommates or friend group? How can you show love to your family? What is God asking you to focus on today?

DEAR LORD, I CAN BE SO SELFISH AT TIMES. OPEN MY EYES TO FOCUS ON THOSE AROUND ME SO I CAN PURPOSEFULLY LOVE THEM. IN JESUS' NAME, AMEN.

A Sweet Conviction

Do not rejoice when your enemy meets trouble.
Let there be no gladness when he falls.
PROVERBS 24:17 TLB

Can we admit this is hard *not* to do? If we were honest, we'd confess it can sometimes feel like poetic justice when someone meets troubling times. We can find ourselves secretly celebrating when they fall. We may even snicker as they land in the pit of despair. Friend, this is why we need Jesus.

Left alone in our human condition, we are wretched. Jealousy and envy highlight our self-seeking tendencies and our unloving responses toward others. But once we become believers of Jesus, a transformation takes place. We may still have those mean-spirited feelings, but the Holy Spirit brings a sweet conviction and empowers us to make loving choices instead. We willingly extend a helping hand, even to those who treat us badly. We learn to show genuine concern rather than gloating at their demise.

DEAR LORD, THANK YOU FOR THE HOLY SPIRIT'S TRANSFORMATIVE WORK IN MY LIFE. IN JESUS' NAME, AMEN.

Building One Another Up

We who are strong in the faith ought to help the weak to carry their burdens. We should not please ourselves. Instead, we should all please other believers for their own good, in order to build them up in the faith.

ROMANS 15:1–2 GNT

We love one another by standing together in community, helping each other carry the weight of the burdens of life. There will be times when we're the strong ones and other times we'll be the ones who desperately need help. The idea is that we stand in unity with our community. We show devotion to each other.

Be quick to bring encouragement through a kind word or a powerful scripture. Let compassion drive your responses and actions. Be Jesus with skin as you reach out and offer your heartfelt support. Let all be done to build each other up in the faith.

DEAR LORD, I APPRECIATE THE GIFT OF COMMUNITY AND HOW WE WORK TOGETHER IN LOVE TO BRING ENCOURAGEMENT. USE ME IN POWERFUL WAYS! IN JESUS' NAME, AMEN.

Family Love

And now this word to all of you: You should be like one big happy family, full of sympathy toward each other, loving one another with tender hearts and humble minds.

1 PETER 3:8 TLB

No matter how you slice it, family is messy. Whether it's blood relations or one pieced together with friends, there are times it's challenging to interact like one big happy family. But God's desire is that we embrace others with love, fueled by tenderness and humility.

Of course there will be arguments. Frustrations will come into play. We'll battle jealousy and feelings of rejection. There will be moments where we're annoyed and want to be left alone. But at the end of the day, love should be what holds us together. We extend grace and embrace restoration because that's what families who genuinely love each other do. Ask God to help you walk this out.

DEAR LORD, HELP ME BE A THOUGHTFUL FAMILY MEMBER WHO SEES THE VALUE IN OTHERS AND FIGHTS TO CREATE A HEALTHY COMMUNITY. IN JESUS' NAME, AMEN.

Showing Kindness Instead

Don't repay evil for evil. Don't snap back at those who say unkind things about you. Instead, pray for God's help for them, for we are to be kind to others, and God will bless us for it.

1 PETER 3:9 TLB

Scripture is clear that when your sister lashes out in anger, your boss demeans you in the meeting, or your friend gossips behind your back, we're not to respond the same way, even though we may feel like it! Instead, our posture should be one of kindness. Our response should be based in love. It may take a minute or two to find our bearings, but we can trust that when we show love in those hurtful situations, the Lord will bless our obedience.

We can also set healthy boundaries and advocate for ourselves, but repaying evil for evil should never be part of our lives as believers.

DEAR LORD, HELP ME KEEP MY MOUTH SHUT WHEN I WANT TO SNAP BACK. EMPOWER ME TO BE KIND INSTEAD. IN JESUS' NAME, AMEN.

Aligning

If you want a happy, good life, keep control of your tongue, and guard your lips from telling lies.

1 PETER 3:10 TLB

It's important that words and actions align. When we tell someone that we love them, but our actions don't convey it, others struggle to believe what we say is true. Our words seem disingenuous. Telling them they're precious but then screaming for a mistake is confusing. Saying we care but then giving them the silent treatment for a bad choice are polar opposites. If we truly care for others, then we'll walk that out in how we treat them.

That's not to say we're perfect and won't ever use hurtful words. There are times when our tongue seems to have a mind of its own. But as believers, we can pray for the strength and wisdom to know when to speak and when to remain silent. We can ask God to help us speak with compassion and truth so we can experience peace.

DEAR LORD, HELP MY WORDS AND ACTIONS ALIGN. IN JESUS' NAME, AMEN.

When It Feels Impossible

Turn away from evil and do good. Try to live in peace even if you must run after it to catch and hold it! For the Lord is watching his children, listening to their prayers; but the Lord's face is hard against those who do evil.

1 PETER 3:11–12 TLB

God commands us to love others. He wants us to make the right choices that promote peace with those around us. But He knows there are times we must dig in deep and find the grit to do so. It's not easy, and people sometimes make expressing kindness and generosity feel impossible. We need God's strength to show compassion and extend grace when we'd rather unleash our honest thoughts and feelings.

Where are your limits of compassion being stretched? Where does peace feel unreachable? Pray. Tell God and let Him reveal the next right step. Ask for help and guidance. He will empower you to do His will every time.

DEAR LORD, I CANNOT LOVE OTHERS WELL WITHOUT YOUR HELP. IN JESUS' NAME, AMEN.

Clothed in Genuine Love

Don't focus on decorating your exterior by doing your hair or putting on fancy jewelry or wearing fashionable clothes; let your adornment be what's inside—the real you, the lasting beauty of a gracious and quiet spirit, in which God delights.

1 PETER 3:3–4 VOICE

Too often, we worry more about how we look on the outside than what's on the inside. We want to look put together, so we invest in our clothes and hair. We put effort into our skincare routine and products. We are freshly manicured and pedicured. We exercise to help keep a youthful and fit appearance. Rather than focusing on a gracious attitude toward others, we focus on ourselves. Instead, let's clothe ourselves in love.

Scripture says that God delights in righteous living. Our desire should be to grow in our faith and be more like Christ. As we're purposeful to clothe ourselves in genuine love for others, the Lord will be glorified as we show compassion.

DEAR LORD, I DESIRE TO GROW MORE LIKE CHRIST. IN JESUS' NAME, AMEN.

Love Isn't Always Convenient

Don't let selfishness and prideful agendas take over. Embrace true humility, and lift your heads to extend love to others. Get beyond yourselves and protecting your own interests; be sincere, and secure your neighbors' interests first.

PHILIPPIANS 2:3–4 VOICE

Selfishness has no place in the lives of believers, and pride keeps us from being effective for the kingdom. When our biggest concern is being comfortable and cared for, we lose sight of those around us. We become number one, and the needs of others fall down the list of importance. Friend, this is not okay with God.

Loving people isn't always convenient. It requires us to set aside our desires so we can invest in their needs. It means giving up a quiet weekend to watch a friend's kids. It means cutting back on your entertainment expenses to help pay their medical bills. And it means opening your home to someone who needs a temporary place to stay. Extend love to others.

DEAR LORD, SHOW ME HOW TO LOVE SELFLESSLY. IN JESUS' NAME, AMEN.

Let's Shine like Stars

Do everything without complaining or arguing, so that you may be innocent and pure as God's perfect children, who live in a world of corrupt and sinful people. You must shine among them like stars lighting up the sky, as you offer them the message of life.

PHILIPPIANS 2:14–16 GNT

God's Word trains us to live in ways that glorify Him and are good for us. It teaches us how to live with compassion for the broken world and be agents of unity and peace. The scriptures reveal what matters most to the Lord and renew our minds for righteous living. As we strive to follow His commands and grow in our faith, we end up shining Jesus to those around us. His love works through our obedience.

Let's be women who refuse to grumble about what life brings our way. Let's not be known as argumentative. Instead, let's show kindness and generosity even when we think others don't deserve it.

DEAR LORD, SHOW ME HOW TO BE A BLESSING. IN JESUS' NAME, AMEN.

Brag and Boast

There is no one like Timothy. What sets him apart from others is his deep concern for you and your spiritual journey. This is rare, my friends.
PHILIPPIANS 2:20 VOICE

We have the opportunity to show love through authentic compliments. Not only do they bring much-needed encouragement at the right times, but a kind word can strengthen someone to follow God's calling on their life. They can also instill a sense of confidence in the hearts of others. Paul demonstrates this in his letter above. He spoke highly of Timothy and let the church know what set him apart from others. His kind and accurate words bless both Timothy and the readers.

Look for these opportunities in your life. Embrace every chance to compliment someone for who they are, their good choices, or a job well done. Brag and boast with honesty about others. Let them know you see their goodness.

DEAR LORD, HELP ME BE QUICK TO BRAG AND BOAST ABOUT OTHERS IN WAYS THAT BUILD THEM UP AND CREATE CONFIDENCE. IN JESUS' NAME, AMEN.

Embrace every chance to compliment someone for who they are, their good choices, or a job well done.

How We Treat Others

Never speak sharply to an older man, but plead with him respectfully just as though he were your own father. Talk to the younger men as you would to much-loved brothers. Treat the older women as mothers, and the girls as your sisters, thinking only pure thoughts about them.

1 TIMOTHY 5:1–2 TLB

The words we say and how we act reveal the condition of our hearts. That's why it's important to be thoughtful in our treatment of others. We want to show respect and respond with kindness whenever possible. Whether older or younger, people deserve to be handled with care. We demonstrate our love when we do.

How does this challenge you? Where can you make some changes? How can you express a heart of compassion to those around you? Maybe pick up the tab at lunch, speak encouragement, or help them think through tough decisions. Open the door, bake their favorite treat, or listen to their stories. Just love them.

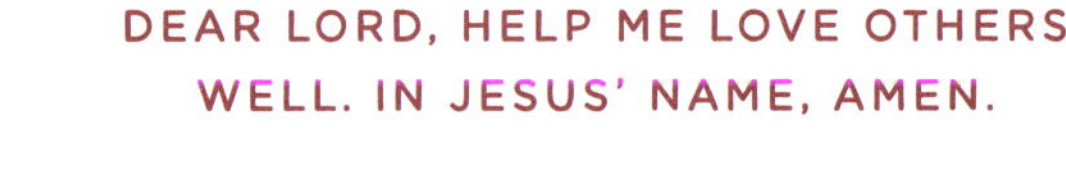

Loving Family

But anyone who won't care for his own relatives when they need help, especially those living in his own family, has no right to say he is a Christian. Such a person is worse than the heathen.

1 Timothy 5:8 TLB

We're called to love our family in meaningful ways. Be it immediate or extended, God's plan is that we meet their needs as best as we can. Sometimes, that is easy, and other times, it requires a sacrifice.

But how do we do this when we're at odds with a family member? What if they were abusive growing up or are dismissive now? What if they pile on guilt and shame at every turn? What if they regularly take their anger out on us? At times, and with some people, choosing to love takes God's strength to walk out. Be in prayer, asking Him to work through you and enable you to obey His command to love in healthy ways.

DEAR LORD, WHEN I CAN'T
MUSTER THE STRENGTH TO LOVE,
PLEASE HELP ME. IN JESUS' NAME, AMEN.

Without Favoritism

Remember that the Lord draws no distinction between Jew and non-Jew—He is Lord over all things, and He pours out His treasures on all who invoke His name.

ROMANS 10:12 VOICE

If God doesn't show favoritism in how He views people, we shouldn't either. There's no good reason to love certain groups but hate others. Everyone deserves to be treated kindly, even if we think differently than they do. Oftentimes, we can only accomplish this high calling through God's enabling.

Let's be women who deliberately clothe ourselves in love, showing kindness and generosity regardless of another's political party or religious beliefs. Can't we agree to disagree and still respect each other? Let's show compassion to those who look different, live differently, and express themselves in different ways. God made each of us on purpose and for a purpose. Let's choose to accept His handiwork without prejudice.

DEAR LORD, I AM INCLINED TO SHOW FAVORITISM AND NEED YOU TO SHOW ME HOW TO LOVE WITHOUT DISTINCTION. IN JESUS' NAME, AMEN.

Love Works on Many Levels

What you do to serve others not only provides for the needs of God's people, but also produces more and more prayers of thanksgiving to God. You will honor God through this genuine act of service because of your commitment to spread the Good News of Christ and because of your generosity in sharing with them and everyone else.

2 CORINTHIANS 9:12–13 GW

Have you ever considered that your acts of love toward those around you increase the praise the Lord receives? We know our compassion blesses others and points to God's goodness, but scripture reminds us that it also produces more prayers of thanksgiving. This directly delights the heart of the Father in ways we cannot comprehend.

When we act with care and concern, it works on many levels. It benefits the one on the receiving end, we feel a divine reward for selflessness, and God is honored. It's a win-win-win scenario. Knowing that, let's love with abandon.

DEAR LORD, LET LOVE REIGN IN MY HEART! IN JESUS' NAME, AMEN.

Cheerful Givers

Giving grows out of the heart—otherwise, you've reluctantly grumbled "yes" because you felt you had to or because you couldn't say "no," but this isn't the way God wants it. For we know that "God loves a cheerful giver."

2 CORINTHIANS 9:7 VOICE

Today's verse is a call to check our motives. It's a challenge to make sure we're stepping out in compassion for all the right reasons. If our heart isn't in the right place, God will know it, and our best efforts will fall flat. He wants us to be cheerful givers of our time and treasure. To the Lord, love is a matter of the heart and an act of obedience rather than something we reluctantly do to check a box.

Time in prayer and the Word will help make it possible to extend genuine love. It will help us determine if our motivation is pure or polluted.

DEAR LORD, HELP ME LOVE OUT OF MY HEART AND NOT BECAUSE OF OBLIGATION. IN JESUS' NAME, AMEN.

Overwhelmed by Blessings

God is ready to overwhelm you with more blessings than you could ever imagine so that you'll always be taken care of in every way and you'll have more than enough to share.

2 Corinthians 9:8 VOICE

Out of God's immeasurable love for you, blessings are coming. Some of them you've experienced or are enjoying right now, but others are in the works and will be in His perfect timing. They might be answers to prayer or a divine surprise you never expected. But you can trust God will show abundant compassion and provide for all your needs.

To show your love in return, commit to a righteous life. Know what His commands say and choose daily to follow them with passion and purpose. Make the effort to grow closer through time in the Word and prayer. Your devotion and dedication will speak volumes to the Lord and delight His heart.

DEAR LORD, THANK YOU FOR LOVING ME IN MIRACULOUS WAYS. HELP ME LOVE YOU IN FAITHFUL ONES. IN JESUS' NAME, AMEN.

When Loving Parents Is Hard

"Respect your father and your mother."
MATTHEW 19:19 GNT

For some, showing love and respect to your parents is easy because your childhood was magical. There were ups and downs, but you felt safe and secure. You felt valued. You knew tough times would pass, and their love for you was solid. As you look back, growing up was a good season of life.

Others, however, experienced the exact opposite. They lacked a loving home and a feeling of security. Their childhood was filled with abuse and neglect, rejection and abandonment, or a mixture of them all. So how can they respect their parents? This is something only accomplished through God.

If this is you, talk to the Lord. Let Him help you navigate the complexities and find healing. Let Him direct your steps toward forgiveness or restoration. With wisdom, define healthy boundaries. Trust that God will show you how to love difficult parents and honor them in the right ways.

DEAR LORD, LEAD ME TO RESPECT MY PARENTS. IN JESUS' NAME, AMEN.

Loving Through Listening

Listen, open your ears, harness your desire to speak, and don't get worked up into a rage so easily, my brothers and sisters.

JAMES 1:19 VOICE

We can show compassion toward others by simply allowing them space to talk. Listening with intention lets them know they matter and what they have to say is valued. Too often, we jump in with our thoughts or opinions. We interrupt as we try to defend ourselves. Rather than let them say everything that needs to be said, our anger boils over and into the conversation.

What if we decided to walk out today's verse in every conversation? What if we opened our ears to what's on their heart, even if it's difficult to hear? What if we showed love by offering our undivided attention? When people muster the courage to speak, what if we honored them by harnessing our desire to speak?

DEAR LORD, HELP ME CLOSE MY MOUTH AND OPEN MY EARS SO OTHERS ARE ENCOURAGED TO SHARE WHAT'S ON THEIR HEART. IN JESUS' NAME, AMEN.

God Gives Lovingly

If you don't have all the wisdom needed for this journey, then all you have to do is ask God for it; and God will grant all that you need. He gives lavishly and never scolds you for asking.

JAMES 1:5 VOICE

God's love is demonstrated by His willingness to supply us with what we need according to His plan and timing. He cares. While we may be embarrassed or worried about asking our huge God for things that seem small in comparison, He deeply values those prayers. The Lord loves to hear from us with all calibers of challenges and difficulties.

Friend, what do you need today? Are you lacking wisdom or discernment? Maybe it's a financial path forward? Are you hoping for emotional or physical healing? Do you need courage or confidence to step out of your comfort zone? Are you short on patience or long on suffering? All you have to do is ask.

DEAR LORD, THANKS FOR HEARING MY REQUESTS AND ANSWERING ACCORDING TO YOUR PERFECT PLAN AND TIMING. IN JESUS' NAME, AMEN.

Divine Assignments of His Love

We have a special role in His plan. He calls us to life by His message of truth so that we will show the rest of His creatures His goodness and love.

JAMES 1:18 VOICE

As believers, we're privileged to reveal God's love to others through how we treat them. Our words have the power to show His goodness to a broken world. When we step out in faith to comfort or help, our actions point to the Lord in heaven. He will open doors and provide opportunities to be His hands and feet to those needing help or hope.

It may be hard to believe God created you for this special role, but He did. You are part of His plan to bless others in His name. But it requires your willingness and obedience. Don't miss a divine assignment and the blessings that flow from it.

DEAR LORD, EMPOWER ME TO WALK OUT DIVINE ASSIGNMENTS TO SHOW YOUR LOVE AND GOODNESS TO THE WORLD. IN JESUS' NAME, AMEN.

Let's be women who put the Word into motion and demonstrate God's love to the world.

Putting the Word into Action

Put the word into action. If you think hearing is what matters most, you are going to find you have been deceived.

James 1:22 voice

We are called as believers to put into action what God commands us to do in the Bible. If it tells us to love, we must show compassion to those around us. If the Word tells us to forgive, we should extend grace to those who offend us. If the Lord's will is that we share the gospel, feed the hungry, and clothe the poor, we should focus our time, talents, and treasure in obedient action.

Faith with feet is God's expectation. His plan is for believers to reveal His love to the lost and dying world through action. We're to engage with others, revealing His goodness by how we treat people. Let's be women who put the Word into motion and demonstrate God's love to the world.

DEAR LORD, LET ME HEAR YOUR WORD AND WALK IT OUT DAILY IN LOVE. IN JESUS' NAME, AMEN.

Taking Care of Them

The Christian who is pure and without fault, from God the Father's point of view, is the one who takes care of orphans and widows, and who remains true to the Lord—not soiled and dirtied by his contacts with the world.

JAMES 1:27 TLB

God is greatly moved when believers take meaningful and significant steps to care for the disenfranchised. When on earth, Jesus was drawn to the sick and lost and focused on helping and healing them. His heart was tendered toward the widow and orphan, demonstrating His love for them countless times. So, when we take up that mantle of care today, it speaks volumes to the Father. Our compassion doesn't go unnoticed.

Let the plight of those around you tender your heart. Look for opportunities to care for those needing extra attention. Be purposeful to meet their needs and passionate as you express care and concern.

DEAR LORD, LET MY HEART BREAK
FOR WHAT BREAKS YOUR HEART,
AND LET IT MOVE ME INTO ACTION.
IN JESUS' NAME, AMEN.

Good and Godly Community

Do not be fooled. "Bad companions ruin good character."

1 CORINTHIANS 15:33 GNT

The people you hang out with reflect who you are. If you spend time with people who focus only on themselves and their needs, you will too. If you surround yourself with friends who are chasing after the things of the world, you will too. And if your tribe is people who point you to earthly solutions rather than to the eternal God, that will become your DEFAULT button. Be careful!

The goal of the Christian life is to love the Lord with all your heart, mind, and strength and love your neighbor as yourself. Knowing that, create community with those who have the same aspiration. Use discernment and wisdom as you make friends so you can trust them to offer godly encouragement when life gets complicated. Commit to being that kind of friend in return. Your character matters to God, so make choices that promote compassion.

DEAR LORD, HELP ME CREATE A GOOD AND GODLY COMMUNITY. IN JESUS' NAME, AMEN.

When We Forgive

"If a believer sins, correct him. If he changes the way he thinks and acts, forgive him. Even if he wrongs you seven times in one day and comes back to you seven times and says that he is sorry, forgive him."

LUKE 17:3–4 GW

Let's be honest: This verse challenges even the most seasoned believer. Forgiving someone once can be challenging, but doing so repeatedly can feel almost impossible. We expect change to happen, and when it doesn't, we get to the end of our rope. God expects more from us. We're to extend grace for every apology. But why?

When we forgive, it's as much for our benefit as theirs. It releases us from replaying the hurt in our minds. It keeps us from obsessing over the offense. Our forgiveness demonstrates love for them and, at the same time, provides us with freedom.

DEAR LORD, EMPOWER ME TO EXTEND GRACE, NO MATTER HOW DIFFICULT IT FEELS. HELP ME SEE THE BIGGER PICTURE OF WHAT FORGIVENESS PROVIDES. IN JESUS' NAME, AMEN.

Respect and Humility

You who are younger in the faith: do as your elders and leaders ask. All of you should treat each other with humility, for as it says in Proverbs, God opposes the proud but offers grace to the humble.

1 PETER 5:5 VOICE

When we treat someone with respect and humility, it's an act of love. Not only for that person but also for the Lord because in doing so, we obey His commands. According to scripture, we'll be blessed by God.

Let's be kind to those in authority over us, listening and following their suggestions. These elders and leaders have acquired hard-won wisdom and have been put into lofty positions by the Lord. Let's show honor to those who've walked this life of faith longer than we have. They helped clear the pathways we're now traversing on our own personal faith journey. Their faithfulness helps bolster ours. God tells us to treat them with kindness. Let's be women who do.

DEAR LORD, EMPOWER ME TO SHOW RESPECT AND HUMILITY TO OTHERS. IN JESUS' NAME, AMEN.

Caring for the Flock

Feed the flock of God; care for it willingly,
not grudgingly; not for what you will get out of it but
because you are eager to serve the Lord. Don't be
tyrants, but lead them by your good example.
1 PETER 5:2–3 TLB

We all have a *flock* to care for—one God has called us to. It could be a small group you lead at church or being the emotional support for your friends. Maybe you're the glue that holds your family together or the volunteer coordinator at your favorite charity. Regardless, take this responsibility to heart and care for it willingly because it delights the Lord and ultimately brings Him glory.

You may feel frustrated sometimes that you're always the one to oversee everything. It's challenging when others automatically look to you for answers and details. But, friend, this is a beautiful opportunity to love others with a generous spirit, just like God has commanded.

DEAR LORD, HELP ME LOVE MY FLOCK WELL
AND WITH JOY. IN JESUS' NAME, AMEN.

In This Together

Be alert, be on watch! Your enemy, the Devil, roams around like a roaring lion, looking for someone to devour. Be firm in your faith and resist him, because you know that other believers in all the world are going through the same kind of sufferings.

1 Peter 5:8–9 GNT

We're all in this together. As believers, we're facing hardships of every kind. If you've ever doubted this, let today's verses be a firm confirmation of the fact. The devil is doing all he can to destroy and discourage, and throughout the world, we're all feeling the heat. It's unavoidable. But we can stand firm in our faith, pressing into the Lord for strength and perseverance.

You can be an encouragement and support to those around you. Be the voice of reason when others are struggling. Be the one who points back to the Lord, reminding them they're not alone. Show compassion as you help them navigate the storms.

DEAR LORD, USE ME IN MIGHTY WAYS TO ENCOURAGE OTHERS AND POINT THEM TO YOU. IN JESUS' NAME, AMEN.

The Attached Promise

Children, it is your Christian duty to obey your parents, for this is the right thing to do. "Respect your father and mother" is the first commandment that has a promise added: "so that all may go well with you, and you may live a long time in the land."

EPHESIANS 6:1–3 GNT

Aha! Did you catch that? There's a powerful reason to show our parents respect through obedience. It's not for nothing. When we choose to honor them, as God commands, we are rewarded for it. There's a robust promise attached that provides a significant reason to treat our mom and dad with kindness. Our devotion enables us to experience God's goodness.

That's not the only reason we want to love our parents well, but it's a substantial incentive that offers a win for everyone. Even as we grow up, even though they weren't and aren't perfect, we can still respect them and hold them dear.

DEAR LORD, THANK YOU FOR MY PARENTS. HELP ME LOVE THEM WELL. IN JESUS' NAME, AMEN.

As If

Don't obey them only while you're being watched, as if you merely wanted to please people. But obey like slaves who belong to Christ, who have a deep desire to do what God wants them to do. Serve eagerly as if you were serving your heavenly master and not merely serving human masters.

EPHESIANS 6:6–7 GW

This is a reminder to live authentically, more concerned with doing what's right in God's eyes than looking good to others. When your heart is in sync with His, your motives will also line up. You won't be overly concerned with pleasing people because your deepest desire will be to please the Lord. When you serve others with the same integrity as if you were directly serving Him, it's an act of love. They are honored, and so is the Lord.

The next time you're struggling, think about the bigger picture. Let God be your focus as you serve and work.

DEAR LORD, LET ME SERVE OTHERS AS IF I'M SERVING YOU! IN JESUS' NAME, AMEN.

Praying About Anything and Everything

Pray always. Pray in the Spirit. Pray about everything in every way you know how! And keeping all this in mind, pray on behalf of God's people. Keep on praying feverishly, and be on the lookout until evil has been stayed.

Ephesians 6:18 voice

When you pray, you're telling God that you believe in Him. It's a vote of confidence in His abilities. Your honest and raw prayers deepen your relationship because it signals your reliance. We usually only share those hard moments and overwhelming fears with those we trust the most. God is blessed whenever we cry out for His help or praise His faithful response.

You are deeply loved by the one who created you. Show your love to Him through regular conversations about anything and everything, anytime. Be it a broken relationship, a tough day at work, or a front-row parking place in the rain, He's listening.

DEAR LORD, WHAT A GIFT
TO TALK TO YOU ANYTIME.
I LOVE YOU! IN JESUS' NAME, AMEN.

A Peaceful Heart

Try to be at peace with everyone, and try to live a holy life, because no one will see the Lord without it.

HEBREWS 12:14 GNT

The idea of peace sounds wonderful, but finding it and holding on to it takes intentionality. It's not something we come by easily. It's not usually our DEFAULT button. But for believers, peace is always available when we need it. It's something God wants to reign in our lives every day and in every way. As we interact with peaceful hearts in our relationships, others will feel loved and cared for.

How are you doing with this? Are you being tossed about by chaotic circumstances, or is the peace of Jesus at work? Are you a calming force for others, bringing a godly perspective to trying times? Are you a place of comfort when someone is struggling? A peaceful heart is yours for the asking. It will bless you and enable you to be a blessing to another.

DEAR LORD, GIVE ME A PEACEFUL HEART. IN JESUS' NAME, AMEN.

Looking After Each Other

Look after each other so that not one of you will fail to find God's best blessings. Watch out that no bitterness takes root among you, for as it springs up it causes deep trouble, hurting many in their spiritual lives.

HEBREWS 12:15 TLB

Good friends and family are a blessing! The truth is that we need each other so we can stay strong and encouraged as we walk through life. We need others to show us where they see God moving in our circumstances. We need to be challenged when we're digging in our heels about the wrong things. We need to be reminded to keep short accounts rather than cling to unforgiveness. We desperately need good and godly community. . .and others need us too.

Let's be women who look after each other. We can commit to being present in one another's lives, always pointing to God and His goodness. Let's love others with passion and purpose.

DEAR LORD, THANK YOU FOR THE GIFT OF GOOD AND GODLY COMMUNITY! IN JESUS' NAME, AMEN.

We desperately need good and godly community. . .and others need us too.

Discipline Without Discouragement

Have you forgotten the encouraging words which God speaks to you as his children? "My child, pay attention when the Lord corrects you, and do not be discouraged when he rebukes you. Because the Lord corrects everyone he loves, and punishes everyone he accepts as a child."

HEBREWS 12:5–6 GNT

It's uncomfortable and embarrassing to be called out for doing wrong. It can leave us feeling ashamed and unloved. All our walls go up to protect ourselves. Correction can often feel condemning.

But when our Father corrects through His Holy Spirit, it's a conviction that never leaves us feeling broken. Instead, His correction brings a desire to do better and be better. God challenges us because He loves us. We need His guidance to stay on the path of righteousness. So, friend, let the Lord discipline you without feeling any discouragement. He corrects only because He loves, so let His love direct you into holy living.

DEAR LORD, THANK YOU FOR LOVING ME ENOUGH TO REDIRECT MY MISSTEPS. IN JESUS' NAME, AMEN.

Wisdom in Waiting

A fool does not think before he unleashes his temper,
but a wise man holds back and remains quiet.
PROVERBS 29:11 VOICE

It is not only wise to hold our tongue; it's an act of love. Too often, our first inclination is to react with the full force of our feelings behind it. We want to go nuclear, saying what's on our mind, knowing it could inflict pain on another. At that moment, we don't care. We are angry and hurt and want them to feel the same.

Instead, God tells us to remain quiet. It's in those crucial moments of silence that we pray for perspective. We ask for peace. We let God give us the right words so we can respond lovingly and firmly. Rather than react, we gather our thoughts as He settles our spirit. There is wisdom in waiting to speak. When we do, it shows compassion to others.

DEAR LORD, HELP ME REMEMBER TO REMAIN QUIET WHEN I WANT TO SPEAK OUT QUICKLY IN ANGER. IN JESUS' NAME, AMEN.

Genuine Friends

There are "friends" who pretend to be friends,
but there is a friend who sticks closer than a brother.
PROVERBS 18:24 TLB

Let's be women who genuinely love our friends. Let's express honest care and concern instead of pretending to care or trying to manipulate to get what we want. The world is full of disingenuous people who see relationships as expendable when they no longer benefit them. They befriend others to give them social clout or to help in some selfish way. It hurts when the truth is revealed.

Community is important, and God designed it to help us navigate the hills and valleys of life. He gives us friends to offer encouragement when our circumstances feel overwhelming. They point us to the Lord to see His goodness. They act as His hands and feet, bringing help and hope. They love without condemnation or judgment. Let's be these kinds of friends.

DEAR LORD, BLESS ME WITH GENUINE FRIENDSHIPS AND HELP ME BE THE SAME KIND OF FRIEND IN RETURN. IN JESUS' NAME, AMEN.

We're to Love Instead

But here is the even harder truth: anyone who is angry with his brother will be judged for his anger. Anyone who taunts his friend, speaks contemptuously toward him, or calls him "Loser" or "Fool" or "Scum," will have to answer to the high court. And anyone who calls his brother a fool may find himself in the fires of hell.

MATTHEW 5:22 VOICE

We are to keep short accounts of wrongs. There's no place in scripture that says otherwise. As humans, our sinful nature may demand that we hold a grudge. It may tell us to speak what's on our mind without a filter. It may encourage us to stay angry and hold it over another. But friend, that isn't an expression of love. God calls us to love without fail.

What is the Holy Spirit speaking to you right now? Where are you being challenged to change? How do you need God's help to love better?

DEAR LORD, CHANGE MY HEART SO I CAN LOVE AS YOU COMMANDED. IN JESUS' NAME, AMEN.

Choose a Tender Answer

A tender answer turns away rage, but a prickly reply spikes anger.

PROVERBS 15:1 VOICE

Sometimes, it's hard to respond in love. We may be tired and cranky. There may be a lot of stuff going on, and we may feel overwhelmed. Maybe we're responding in the same manner as they spoke to us, so it only seems fair. Maybe we think they deserve our wrath or want to make a point by using unkind and harsh words. There might be a million other reasons we're emotionally at the end of our rope. But God wants us to choose a tender answer rather than a prickly reply.

In these moments, take a minute before you speak. Breathe deep and pray for the right words. Call for a timeout and finish the conversation when you've settled down. Do whatever it takes to ensure you love others with your words. Once they're said, you can't take them back.

DEAR LORD, GIVE ME THE ABILITY TO CHOOSE A TENDER ANSWER RATHER THAN A PRICKLY REPLY. IN JESUS' NAME, AMEN.

Going Right to the One

This is what you do if one of your brothers or sisters sins against you: go to him, in private, and tell him just what you perceive the wrong to be. If he listens to you, you've won a brother.

MATTHEW 18:15 VOICE

Before you share your hurt and anger with others, go to the person who offended you. Pray, and then go right to the source of your pain and talk to them. Be honest and open about their actions. Let them know how you are feeling. Work it out between yourselves. If you have genuine love and respect, reconciliation will eventually follow.

Too often, we get hurt and tell others about it immediately. We share our side of the story and badmouth the one who has caused us pain. This isn't how we love our offender. Instead, let's extend grace, walk out today's verse, and trust God for restoration.

DEAR LORD, HELP ME SHOW LOVE BY GOING RIGHT TO THE SOURCE OF MY HURT. IN JESUS' NAME, AMEN.

The Power of Community

And this: if two or three of you come together as a community and discern clearly about anything, My Father in heaven will bless that discernment. For when two or three gather together in My name, I am there in the midst of them.

MATTHEW 18:19–20 VOICE

Today's verses reveal the power of community. Throughout the Word, you'll find countless reminders that there is goodness in togetherness. God honors it with His presence, empowering believers to discern and blessing them for it.

Who is your community? Who are the godly friends you lean on? Who in your family do you trust the most in the hard moments? Where do you go when life begins to unravel? Who stands with you in the lean times and offers sound wisdom for moving forward? Who are the ones you know will pray when asked? Today, thank God for surrounding you with a wonderful community of loving friends and family.

DEAR LORD, THANK YOU FOR THE GIFT OF COMMUNITY AND FOR BLESSING ME IN IT! IN JESUS' NAME, AMEN.

Loving Through Forgiveness

Then Peter came to Jesus and asked him, "Lord, how often do I have to forgive a believer who wrongs me? Seven times?" Jesus answered him, "I tell you, not just seven times, but seventy times seven."

MATTHEW 18:21–22 GW

Gulp. It's hard enough to forgive once, much less endlessly. But that's what Jesus meant when He said seventy times seven. As believers, we're to forgive as an act of love. We're to keep short accounts of wrongs. We are to extend grace and live at peace with others whenever possible.

This matters because doing so keeps us free from the bondage of unforgiveness. Keeping a scorecard of offenses steals our joy. We end up replaying the hurts over and over again, and it leaves us bitter and angry. But when we forgive others, we demonstrate love. We show love to God by obeying His command. We love ourselves by refusing to let unforgiveness take root in our hearts and disrupt our peace.

DEAR LORD, HELP ME FORGIVE QUICKLY AND THOROUGHLY. IN JESUS' NAME, AMEN.

He Sees the Effort

When a man is trying to please God, God makes even his worst enemies to be at peace with him.
PROVERBS 16:7 TLB

It's your effort to live righteously that delights the Lord, not the perfection of it. Our human condition ensures that we'll never be flawless. But God sees our determination to follow His commands. He recognizes the energy put forth and He feels our love as we try to live in ways that please Him. In response, the Lord blesses us with peace. He brings calm out of chaos into the lives of believers trying to honor Him with their choices and decisions.

There is relief in knowing God's expectations aren't for perfection, because we fall short daily. We're incapable of consistently making all the right moves. He knows our deficiencies and defects better than we do. Yet still the Lord is pleased by our efforts as we try to demonstrate our love by following His ways and will.

DEAR LORD, THANK YOU FOR RECOGNIZING MY EFFORTS TO LIVE RIGHTEOUSLY. IN JESUS' NAME, AMEN.

Setting a Good Example

Titus, you have to set a good example for everyone. Go out of your way to do what is right, speak the truth with the weight and authority that come from an honest and pure life. No one can argue with that. Then your enemies will cower in shame because they have nothing bad to say against us.

Titus 2:7–8 voice

Your life is always on display. When finances become tight, others watch your reaction. They look to see how you manage broken relationships, rejection, health issues, disappointments, and times of fear and worry. Because you are a believer, it's important to remember this so you can set a good example. Let them see your faith rise up. Let them see how you trust in the Lord, His love, and His provision.

It's a privilege to set a good example for others. It's an act of love to live in ways that lead them to a saving faith in Jesus.

DEAR LORD, HELP ME MODEL A ROBUST LIFE OF FAITH. IN JESUS' NAME, AMEN.

As believers. . .we can confidently know a blessing awaits us.

The Blessing That Awaits

But as the Scriptures say, No eye has ever seen and no ear has ever heard and it has never occurred to the human heart all the things God prepared for those who love Him.

1 Corinthians 2:9 VOICE

Be encouraged by today's verse. As believers who try to love God with all our heart, soul, mind, and strength, we can confidently know a blessing awaits us. We cannot imagine how magnificent and impressive it will be. We can't even begin to think it up! Our minds are incapable of it. But it's real, and it's waiting for us. So, until then, we love God and love others as commanded.

How do we do that? We focus on getting to know our Father more through His Word. We talk to Him throughout the day, sharing our challenges and celebrations laced with a heart of gratitude. And we show compassion and care to those around us.

DEAR LORD, HELP ME LOVE AND LIVE WITH EXPECTATION FOR WHAT AWAITS ME. IN JESUS' NAME, AMEN.

About the Author

Carey Scott is an author, speaker, and certified Biblical Life Coach who's honest about her walk with the Lord—stumbles, fumbles, and all. With authenticity and humor, she challenges women to be real, not perfect, and reminds them to trust God as their source above all else. Carey lives in Colorado with her husband and has two grown children who give her plenty of material for writing and speaking. She's surrounded by a wonderful family and group of friends who keep her motivated, real, and humble. You can find her at CareyScott.org.